D1520770

by

JACK B. DENNIS

Assistant Professor of Electrical Engineering
Massachusetts Institute of Technology

Mathematical Programming

and Electrical Networks

Copy 2

Published jointly by

The Technology Press of
The Massachusetts Institute of Technology

and

John Wiley & Sons, Inc., New York

Chapman & Hall, Limited, London

TECHNOLOGY PRESS RESEARCH MONOGRAPHS

NONLINEAR PROBLEMS IN RANDOM THEORY
  By Norbert Wiener

CIRCUIT THEORY OF LINEAR NOISY NETWORKS
  By Hermann A. Haus and Richard B. Adler

MATHEMATICAL PROGRAMMING AND ELECTRICAL NETWORKS
  By Jack B. Dennis

Library of Congress Catalog Card Number: 59-12511

Printed in the United States of America

FOREWORD

There has long been a need in science and engineering for
systematic publication of research studies larger in scope than
a journal article but less ambitious than a finished book. Much
valuable work of this kind is now published only in a semiprivate
way, perhaps as a laboratory report, and so may not find its
proper place in the literature of the field. The present contribution is the third of the Technology Press Research Monographs,
which we hope will make selected timely and important research
studies readily accessible to libraries and to the independent
worker.

J. A. Stratton

PREFACE

The research reported in this volume was undertaken by the author in the spring of 1957 as part of his program toward the Doctor of Science in Electrical Engineering at the Massachusetts Institute of Technology. The Union Carbide Corporation and the United States Army Office of Ordnance Research supported the work, which was carried out at the M. I. T. Center for Operations Research. The freedom of action and generous use of facilities granted by Project Supervisor Professor Philip M. Morse and Assistant Director Dr. Herbert P. Galliher were most helpful in stimulating the research.

Professor Dean Arden, who supervised this research, has gladly given much of his time for enthusiastic discussion of the material. To him I owe a large portion of appreciation for his guidance and encouragement. The interest of Professor Samuel J. Mason in electrical models for network flow problems has also been an inspiration to me. I am also indebted to former Professor William Linvill, who sparked the author's interest in linear programming, and to Dr. William S. Jewell who offered consultation and helpful suggestions.

Jack B. Dennis

April, 1959

iv

CONTENTS

Chapter 1

A NEW POINT OF VIEW ON
MATHEMATICAL PROGRAMMING

Quite recently it has been observed[*] that certain simple linear
programming problems could be solved by setting up an equivalent
electrical network containing voltage sources, current sources,
and ideal diodes. If the voltage and current sources are set to
values corresponding to the data of the programming problem, the
optimal solution may be found by simply measuring currents and
voltages at appropriate points in the network, that is, the electrical network automatically establishes a current distribution
which forms an optimal solution of the programming problem.
The principal objective of this monograph is to explore this sur-
prising relation between mathematical programming and electric
circuit principles to the fullest extent.

One may be tempted to question whether the analogy fundamental to this relationship can add appreciably to our store of knowledge
in the field of mathematical programming. True, one can solve
certain programming problems by setting up electrical models; but
this is probably not a practical means of obtaining useful answers,
especially considering the efficiency with which digital computers
can handle the task. What then is the value of investigating these
electrical models? The answer lies in the fundamental difference
in approach of the operations analyst with regard to an optimization
problem and the electrical scientist studying a circuit. The analyst nearly always speaks in terms of minimization or maximization subject to constraints. The electrical scientist, however, is
merely looking for a distribution of currents and voltages which
satisfies the conditions imposed by the circuit - he rarely thinks
in terms of minimization, and may not even realize that an appropriate extremum principle exists. Thus the most significant value
of the electrical analogy is that it gives us a physical model of
mathematical programming problems as a set of conditions which
must be satisfied (the Lagrangian formulation) rather than the common geometrical picture of minimizing a function over a constraint
set.

----
[*]This observation was a result of informal discussion meetings
on the properties of networks at M.I.T. in the fall of 1956, but
principal credit is due Professors Samuel J. Mason and Dean N.
Arden of the Electrical Engineering Department.

2

Summary of Results

The study of the analogy has produced a varied assortment of interesting consequences. In Chapter 3 it is shown that the solution of any electrical network made up of voltage sources, current sources, ideal diodes, and ideal transformers is equivalent to determining the optimal solution of a linear program. Furthermore, the reverse is also true: Any linear programming problem can be modelled by an electrical network of the four types of elements listed above. The three fundamental theorems of linear programming - concerning duality, existence of solutions, and complementary slackness - each have elegant physical meanings when interpreted with respect to electrical networks.

The addition of linear resistors to the list of electrical elements yields (as is demonstrated in Chapter 3) a more general equivalence between quadratic programs with linear constraints and electrical networks. The statements of duality and existence theorems for quadratic programming are an immediate consequence of this extension of the equivalence. The duality theorem of quadratic programming in turn suggests a duality principle for concave programming which is stated in Chapter 2. These results bridge the gap between the familiar duality relation in linear programming and the duality principle stated by Courant and Hilbert for ordinary constrained minimization problems [5].

Perhaps more important than the theoretical results, the electrical analogy permits a new interpretation of algorithms for obtaining solution of programming problems and points the way to the formulation of some new techniques. In Chapter 4 it is shown that the capacitated network flow problem (a generalization of the well-known transportation problem) can be modelled by an electrical network of voltage sources, current sources, and diodes only. Any distribution of current which meets the conditions imposed by the electrical model indicates the optimal flow pattern for the capacitated flow network. The class of electrical networks containing only diodes and sources is important because methods can be constructed for their solution (as in the case of the transportation problem) in which the only arithmetic operations involved are addition and subtraction. Such an algorithm for solving diode-source networks, and therefore applicable to network flow problems, is presented in Chapter 4. Because this method will solve an arbitrary diode-source network, it will also encompass flow problems in which unit costs may be negative or lower bounds may be placed on the flows. The method is also quite flexible and will allow a previous solution of a network to be used as a starting point for a new solution of the network with different parameter values.

An important idea connected with the diode-source algorithm is the concept of a breakpoint curve: Consider a network of diodes and sources from which two leads are brought for external observation. It is shown in Chapter 3 that the combinations of voltage and current that the network will allow on this pair of leads form a sequence of broken line segments, or a breakpoint curve. The above algorithm is based on a scheme for "tracing" the breakpoint curve of a diode-source network and is related to the method of Ford and Fulkerson for the transportation problem [15]. In Chapter 5 of this monograph a general procedure is formulated for tracing the breakpoint curve observed at a terminal pair of an arbitrary network of diodes, sources, resistors, and ideal transformers. The procedure amounts to a slight alteration of the change of basis rules associated with Dantzig's simplex method [9] for linear programming, and thereby gives a physical model for this iteration procedure.

The breakpoint tracing scheme is applicable to the solution of general linear and quadratic programs. In Chapter 6 two algorithms are formulated which employ the tracing procedure. The first is similar, but not identical, to the simplex method. The second is equivalent to the primal-dual method for linear programming devised by Dantzig, Ford and Fulkerson [10]. This procedure, however, is also applicable to quadratic programs and is then equivalent to a slight generalization of Wolfe's procedure [29].

The final chapter of the monograph is concerned with a procedure for obtaining optimal solutions of general programming problems. Gradient methods have long been in use for minimizing a function of many variables. Recently widespread interest has developed in the extension of gradient methods to minimization problems with inequality constraints, or the general programming problem. The method proposed in Chapter 7 involves computing the direction of steepest descent as that allowable direction which produces the greatest rate of decrease of the objective function. An allowable direction is a direction in which it is permissible to move from the present point without leaving the constraint set. It is shown that this computation involves obtaining the optimal vector of a quadratic programming problem for each steepest descent iteration. This does not imply a prohibitive amount of calculation, since a very good initial solution for the quadratic program is always available from the previous step. This direct determination of the direction of steepest descent appears to offer advantages over other gradient procedures that have been suggested for the general programming problem.

For completeness an introduction to mathematical programming is included in Chapter 2. The conditions for the equivalence of relative and global minima are presented, and the Lagrangian formulation is developed. The special cases of linear and quadratic programming are stated, and the relevant fundamental theorems are given.

4

Notation

The following conventions apply throughout the monograph except in Chapter 4, where matrix notation is not employed.

Lower case letters x, y, ... will represent vector quantities and will be uniformly treated as column matrices. A vector inequality

$$x \geq y \qquad \text{or} \qquad x > y$$

always means that the indicated inequality relationship must hold between each pair of corresponding components of x and y. Rectangular matrices will be represented by capital letters. The individual components of a vector or the columns or elements of a rectangular matrix will be distinguished by numerical subscripts

$$A = [A_1 A_2 \ldots A_n] = \begin{bmatrix} a_{11} & a_{12} & \cdots & a_{1n} \\ a_{21} & a_{22} & & \\ \text{-} & \text{-} & \text{-} & \text{-} \\ a_{m1} & \cdots & & a_{mn} \end{bmatrix}$$

The transpose of a matrix will be indicated by a superscript T. Hence the dot product of two vectors

$$x \cdot y = \sum_i x_i y_i$$

will be written $x^T y$. Sometimes the notation $[x, y]$ will also be used. Occasionally it will be necessary to identify the submatrices of a partitioned matrix or vector. This will be done with upper case subscripts, for instance

$$i = \begin{bmatrix} i_C \\ i_V \\ i_D \end{bmatrix}$$

Scalar quantities will be denoted by lower case Greek letters.

The letter designating a function will indicate whether it is a scalar function or a vector function. Thus $\phi(\eta)$ is a scalar function of a scalar variable, $f(\xi)$ is a vector function of a scalar, $\phi(x)$ is a scalar function of a vector, and $f(x)$ maps vectors into vectors.

The gradient of a scalar function of a vector $\phi(x)$ will be represented by

$$\partial\phi \quad = \quad \begin{bmatrix} \dfrac{\partial\phi}{\partial x_1} \\[2ex] \dfrac{\partial\phi}{\partial x_2} \\[2ex] \cdot \\[1ex] \dfrac{\partial\phi}{\partial x_n} \end{bmatrix}$$

The differential of a map of vectors into vectors $f(x)$ will be denoted by

$$df \quad = \quad \begin{bmatrix} \dfrac{\partial f_1}{\partial x_1} & \dfrac{\partial f_1}{\partial x_2} & \cdot & \cdot & \dfrac{\partial f_1}{\partial x_n} \\[2ex] \dfrac{\partial f_2}{\partial x_1} & \dfrac{\partial f_2}{\partial x_2} & & & \\[2ex] - & - & - & - & - & - \\[2ex] \dfrac{\partial f_m}{\partial x_1} & \cdot & \cdot & \cdot & \dfrac{\partial f_m}{\partial x_n} \end{bmatrix}$$

In Chapter 2 and in the proofs given in the appendices, geometrical interpretations will be made of the mathematical reasoning. As an introduction to the concepts of geometry in many-dimensional space, Appendix A defines some of the geometrical terms used here and in other literature on mathematical programming.

Chapter 2

THE NATURE OF PROGRAMMING PROBLEMS

The General Programming Problem
   The most general type of problem that will be considered in
this monograph is the following: The values of a number of
variables are to be selected so that an objective function is minimized among all choices of values that satisfy a group of inequality constraints on functions of the variables. Mathematically,
the problem may be written as

   General Programming Problem:
      Minimize the objective function

$$\phi(x) \tag{2-1a}$$

      subject to the constraints

   (A) $g(x) \geq 0$

          $x \geq 0 \tag{2-1b}$

In this statement,   x is a column vector (matrix) of n components and g(x) represents the column vector of m functions of x

$$g(x) = \begin{bmatrix} g_1(x) \\ g_2(x) \\ - \\ - \\ g_m(x) \end{bmatrix}$$

Differentiability of $\phi(x)$ and g(x) will be assumed.
   To introduce some terminology which will be used throughout
this work, any vector x which satisfies the constraints 2-1b is
called a feasible vector of the programming problem. The set

6

of all feasible vectors is termed the constraint set of the
problem. A feasible vector which produces as low a value
of the objective function as any other feasible vector is
known as an optimal vector.

The constraint relations 2-1b of a programming problem may
also take one of the following alternate forms

B) $g(x) = 0$ C) $g(x) \geq 0$

      $x \geq 0$ x unrestricted

Simple considerations show that a problem expressed in any
one of the three forms can be expressed in the other two forms.
The principles are: 1) an equality constraint relation can be
replaced by a pair of inequalities, and 2) an unrestricted variable
can be replaced by the difference of two nonnegative variables.
The precise relations between the three forms are given in
Table 2-1.

The usual analytic methods of solving minimization problems
in the presence of constraint equations (solving the constraint
equations, substituting in the objective function, and differentiating, or the Lagrange multiplier technique) do not work with programming problems. These methods do not take account of the
inequality constraints which characterize mathematical programming problems. It does not seem likely that the solution of a
programming problem will ever be expressed in closed analytic
form. However, the Lagrange multipliers, suitably generalized,
play an important role in the theoretical and computational aspects
of programming. The generalized Lagrange multipliers also have
great physical significance as will be evident in later chapters.

Linear and Quadratic Programs

A particularly important special case of the general programming problem is the linear programming problem in which $\phi(x)$
is simply a linear combination of the variables and $g(x)$ is a
linear transformation.

Linear Programming Problem:
Minimize

$$\phi(x) = c^T x$$

with

$$A x \geq b$$

$$x \geq 0$$

Old	New	Formulation of New Problem in Terms of Old		
		$\overline{g}(\overline{x})$	$\overline{\phi}(\overline{x})$	$\overline{x}$
A	B	$g(x) + Iw$	$\phi(x)$	$\begin{bmatrix} x \\ w \end{bmatrix}$
B	A	$\begin{bmatrix} g(x) \\ -g(x) \end{bmatrix}$	$\phi(x)$	x
A	C	$\begin{bmatrix} g(x) \\ Ix \end{bmatrix}$	$\phi(x)$	x
C	A	$g(x^+ - x^-)$	$\phi(x^+ - x^-)$	$\begin{bmatrix} x^+ \\ x^- \end{bmatrix}$ $x = x^+ + x^-$

I = identity matrix of appropriate order

Table 2-1 Relations between problem formulations

Here the constant vector b of the linear transformation has been
moved to the right-hand side of the constraint relations.

A somewhat more general case, and undoubtedly the simplest
form of nonlinear program, is the quadratic program in which the
objective function is a second degree form in the variables.

Quadratic Programming Problem:
Minimize

$$\frac{1}{2} x^T Q x + c^T x$$

with

$$A x \geq b$$

$$x \geq 0$$

These two special cases form the major subject matter of this
monograph, although a technique for solving general programming
problems is proposed in Chapter 7.

One reason for the importance of the two special cases is that there are computational schemes which produce optimal vectors in a small, finite number of iterative steps. The last iteration produces an <u>exact</u> solution of the linear or quadratic program. On the other hand, methods for solving general programming problems only draw nearer to the solution with each iteration; although convergence may be very rapid, the exact solution is never attained in a finite number of steps.

Local and Global Minima: Concavity and Convexity

An important question in mathematical programming concerns when a local minimum is equivalent to a global minimum. To understand these terms, consider the programming problem as being phrased in an n-dimensional space with one coordinate axis for each variable. Then the constraint set of a programming problem consists of a certain group of points in this space. A point yields a <u>local</u> or <u>relative</u> minimum of the objective function if it is in the constraint set and no "nearby point" in the constraint set gives a lower value of the objective function. A point in the constraint set yields a <u>global</u> minimum if no other point in the constraint set gives a lower value of the objective.

Of course, someone looking for the solution of a particular programming problem wants to find a global minimum. Unfortunately the common methods for obtaining solutions are designed to find local minima. Therefore, it is desirable to know in which cases the two are equivalent. The ideas of concave functions and convex sets yield a simple answer to this question.

Let a function of n variables be represented by the $n + 1^{th}$ coordinate of points on a surface in an $n + 1$-dimensional space in which the $n + 1^{th}$ axis is "vertical." The function is <u>concave</u> if the surface representing it is at no point curved downward. More precisely, the straight line segment joining any two points on this surface must at no point lie beneath the surface. This is illustrated in Fig. 2-1. A function will be termed <u>strictly concave</u> if the line segments mentioned above lie above the surface except for their end points. A function is <u>convex</u> if its negative is concave. Note that according to these conventions, the linear function $\phi(x) = c^T x$, which is represented by a hyperplane in $n + 1$-dimensional space, is both concave and convex, but it is neither strictly concave nor strictly convex.

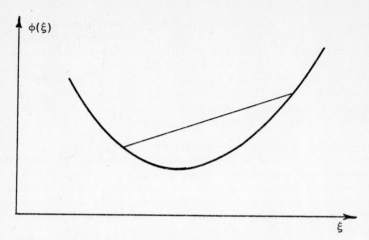

Fig. 2-1 A concave function of a single variable

A <u>convex set</u> is defined as a set of points in n-dimentional space
which contains all points on the line segment joining any two points
in the set. The set of points in n-space for which $\theta(x) > 0$ is a
convex set if θ is a convex function as is indicated in Fig. 2-2. As
an extension of this property, the constraint set of a programming
problem is a convex set if the functions g_1 through g_m are convex,
since this set consists of all points common to the convex sets
determined by each of the g_i (Lemma C-1).

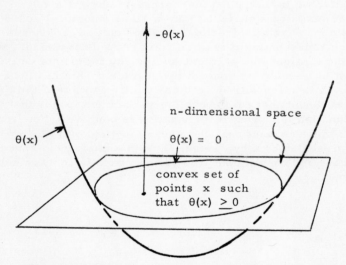

Fig. 2-2 The convex set defined by a convex
function

The important result made possible by these concepts in connection with mathematical programming is the following property
which is proved as Theorem C-1.

For a programming problem with a concave objective function and a convex constraint set, a relative minimum is
also a global minimum.

In the case of the linear programming problem, the objective
function is always concave and the constraint functions are always
convex. It follows that a relative minimum is always a global
minimum in linear programming. With quadratic programming,
the constraint set is likewise convex. However, the objective
function is concave if and only if the matrix Q is positive semidefinite, that is, if $x^T Q x$ is nonnegative for all choices of x (Lemma
D-1). If this is so, then relative and global minima are equivalent
for quadratic programming.

Lagrange Multipliers

Consider the constrained minimization problem

Minimization Problem:

Minimize

$$\phi(x)$$

with

$$g(x) = 0 \qquad\qquad (2\text{-}2b)$$

Following the Lagrange multiplier rule one multiplies each constraint
function g_i by a multiplier $-y_i$ and adds the results to the objective
function to obtain the Lagrangian function

$$\psi(x, y) = \phi(x) - y^T g(x)$$

Differentiating this expression and coupling the result with the constraints 2-2b, one obtains the

Lagrangian Problem:

Find an x and y such that

$$g(x) = 0$$

$$\partial \phi(x) - y^T dg(x) = 0$$

In this statement $\partial \phi$ is the gradient of the objective function and
dg is the differential of the transformation g. The Lagrange
multiplier rule states:

i) If $\bar{x}$ yields a local minimum of ϕ, then there is a vector $\bar{y}$ such that $(\bar{x}, \bar{y})$ is a solution of the Lagrangian problem.

ii) If $(\bar{x}, \bar{y})$ is a solution of the Lagrangian problem, and $\phi(x)$ is concave and the constraint set convex in the vicinity of $\bar{x}$, then $\bar{x}$ yields a relative minimum of ϕ.

Thus the Lagrange multiplier rule gives a second equivalent formulation of any ordinary minimization problem.

The Generalized Lagrangian Problem

In this paragraph the generalization by Kuhn and Tucker [21] of the Lagrange multiplier rule to mathematical programming will be studied. A rigorous proof of the result involves application of the theory of inequalities and is given in Appendix C. However, the reasonableness of the result can be made clear through consideration of some simple cases.

Consider first the simple minimization problem

Minimize $\phi(\xi)$

with $\qquad \xi \geq 0$

As is indicated in Fig. 2-3 two cases are possible. Either the minimum occurs for some $\bar{\xi} > 0$ at which point $\frac{d\phi}{d\xi}(\bar{\xi}) = 0$, or the minimum is at the point $\bar{\xi} = 0$. In the latter case $\frac{d\phi}{d\xi}(0)$ must not be negative. Summarizing this, a necessary condition that $\bar{\xi}$ yield a minimum of $\phi(\xi)$ subject to $\xi \geq 0$ is that

$$\frac{d\phi}{d\xi}(\bar{\xi}) - \bar{\omega} = 0$$

$$\bar{\xi} \geq 0 \qquad \bar{\omega} \geq 0 \qquad\qquad (2\text{-}3b)$$

$$\bar{\omega}\,\bar{\xi} = 0 \qquad\qquad (2\text{-}3c)$$

for some value of $\bar{\omega}$. This is the Lagrangian problem corresponding to the simple minimization problem. The relation 2-3c requires that either $\bar{\xi}$ be zero or $\bar{\omega}$ be zero and hence that only one of the inequalities 2-3b can be satisfied in the strict inequality sense. If $\bar{\xi}$ is greater than zero, $\bar{\omega}$ must be zero and the first case holds; if $\bar{\omega}$ is greater than zero, $\bar{\xi}$ must be zero and the second case holds. Because of this relation between the original inequality restraint and the new one obtained as a necessary condition for a minimum, the relation 2-3c is known as a complementary slackness condition. This condition is related to the behavior of the diode circuit element in electrical networks as will be seen in the next chapter.

a)

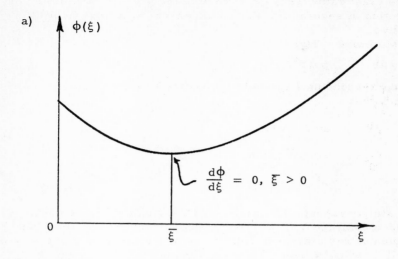

$$\frac{d\phi}{d\xi} = 0, \ \overline{\xi} > 0$$

b)

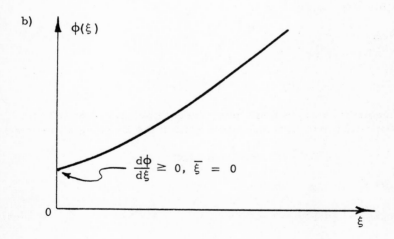

$$\frac{d\phi}{d\xi} \geq 0, \ \overline{\xi} = 0$$

Fig. 2-3 The Lagrangian problem for
unconstrained minimization

The exact same ideas generalize to the problem of minimizing a function of several variables which are constrained to be non-negative.

Minimize $\phi(x)$

with $x \geq 0$

The corresponding Lagrangian problem is to find vectors x and w such that

$$\phi(x) - w = 0$$

$$x \geq 0, \quad w \geq 0$$

$$x^T w = 0$$

This simply repeats the condition of the single variable problem for each component of x in the many variable case. Note that the complementary slackness relation $x^T w = 0$ requires that $x_i w_i = 0$ for all i when x and w are constrained to be nonnegative.

Next a more complicated case will be considered, namely the problem of minimizing a function of two variables subject to a single equality constraint and the condition that the variables be nonnegative.

Minimize $\phi(x) = \phi(x_1, x_2)$

with

$$\theta(x) = \theta(x_1, x_2) = 0$$

$$x_1 \geq 0, \quad x_2 \geq 0$$

If no inequality constraints were present one could find a necessary condition for a minimum by forming the Lagrangian expression

$$\psi(x, \eta) = \phi(x) - \eta \ g(x)$$

and differentiating to obtain

$$\partial \phi(x) - \eta \ \partial \theta(x) = 0 \qquad\qquad (2-4)$$

$$\theta(x) = 0$$

This condition is illustrated geometrically in Fig. 2-4. It requires that at the point $\overline{x}$, the gradient of the objective function must be some multiple η of the gradient of the constraint function.

15

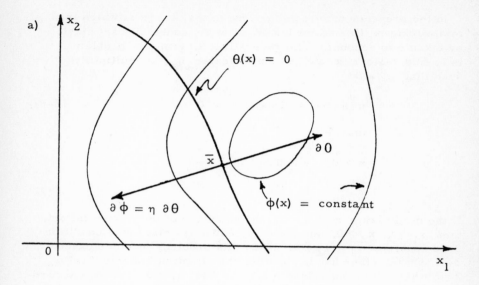

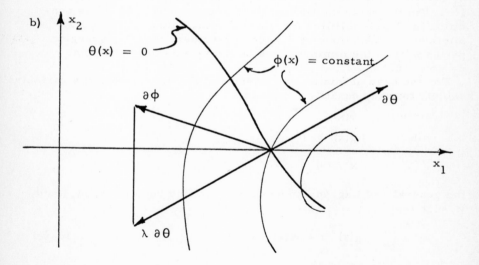

Fig. 2-4 The Lagrangian problem with
a constraint function

16

In the presence of inequality constraints, cases in which the minimizing x lies on the boundary of the constraint set must be taken into account. The generalized Lagrangian problem is to find vectors x and w and a scalar η (the multiplier) such that

$$\eta \, \partial\theta(x) \, - \, \partial\phi(x) + v = 0 \qquad\qquad (2\text{-}5a)$$

$$\theta(x) = 0$$

$$x \geq 0, \quad v \geq 0$$

$$v^T x = 0 \qquad\qquad (2\text{-}5d)$$

If the minimizing x is not on the boundary of the constraint set, then $x_1 > 0$, $x_2 > 0$, and the complementary slackness condition 2-5d requires $v_1 = v_2 = 0$. Then this problem becomes exactly 2-4. On the other hand, consider the situation indicated in Fig. 2-4b where the constrained minimum has $x_1 > 0$, $x_2 = 0$. According to the complementary slackness condition, w_2 may be greater than zero, but w_1 must be equal to zero. Relation 2-5a then states that the x_1 component of $\partial\phi$ must be equal to some multiple of the x_1 component of $\partial\theta$, while the x_2 component of $\partial\phi$ must not be less than the same multiple of the x_2 component of $\partial\theta$. This condition is clearly fulfilled for the case illustrated in the figure. Similar considerations verify the correctness of the Lagrangian problem when the minimum lies on the x_2 axis or at the point $x_1 = x_2 = 0$.

For the case of minimizing a function of many nonnegative variables subject to many equality constraints

Minimize $\phi(x)$

with $g(x) = 0$

              $x \geq 0$

the generalized Lagrangian problem is to find vectors x, y, and v such that

$$dg(x)^T y - \partial\phi(x) + v = 0 \qquad\qquad (2\text{-}6a)$$

$$g(x) = 0$$

$$x \geq 0, \quad v \geq 0$$

$$v^T x = 0$$

These relations have the same form as in the single constraint case with one term for each constraint equation in 2-6a. The form of the Lagrangian problem associated with the general programming problem in the form 2-1 may be found by use of the relations given in Table 2-1. The result is

Generalized Lagrangian Problem:
    Find vectors x, v, u, and y such that

$$dg(x)^T y - \partial\phi(x) + v = 0 \qquad\qquad (2\text{-}7a)$$

$$g(x) - u = 0$$

$$x \geq 0 \qquad v \geq 0 \qquad u \geq 0 \qquad y \geq 0$$

$$v^T x = 0 \qquad\qquad y^T u = 0 \qquad\qquad (2\text{-}7d)$$

The generalized Lagrange multiplier rule (the fundamental theorem for general programming, Theorem D-2) then states:
  i) If x is a locally optimal solution of the general pro-
      gramming problem, then there exist vectors v, u,
      and y such that (x, v, u, y) is a solution of the
      Lagrangian problem.
  ii) If (x, v, u, y) is a solution of the Lagrangian problem
      and $\phi(x)$ is concave and the constraint set convex in the
      vicinity of x , then x yields a relative optimal solu-
      tion of the programming problem.
    A geometric interpretation of the Lagrangian problem can be made if 2-7a is rewritten as

$$\partial\phi(x) = dg(x)^T y + I v \qquad\qquad (2\text{-}8)$$

The columns of the rectangular matrix $dg(x)^T$ are vectors nor-
mal to the constraint surfaces $g_i(x) = 0$ at the point x, and the columns of the identity matrix are vectors normal to the constraint surfaces $x_i = 0$. The relation 2-8 requires that the gradient of the objective function be expressed as a positive linear combination of the normals of the constraint surface. The complementary slackness conditions 2-7d allow only normals to equality satisfied con-
straints to participate in the linear combination. Fig. 2-5 gives an illustration of this principle.

Equivalent Formulations: Duality
    The relation developed above between extremum problems on the one hand and the systems of relations constituting the Lagran-
gian problems on the other is often observed in the physical systems. Moreover, it frequently happens that two distinctly different extremum formulations lead to the very same Lagrangian problem. One

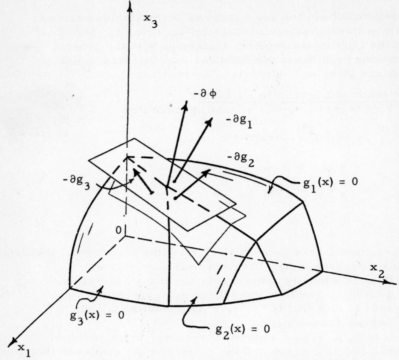

Fig. 2-5 Geometric interpretation of the
Lagrangian problem

group of physical examples where this occurs is the electrical
networks which are studied extensively in the next few chapters.
In such cases, the two extremum formulations are equivalent
in the sense that they both give a complete description of the
same physical situation. For this reason they are said to bear
a dual relationship to each other. The Legendre transformation
has a dominant role in this duality relation. Therefore a digres-
sion will be made to introduce it and its properties.

The Legendre Transformation

In the study of geometry there is a strong dual relationship between points and planes in three-dimensional space or between
points and hyperplanes in a multidimensional space. The specification of a surface in a multidimensional space is one example of
this duality principle. In an n+1 dimensional space, the usual way
of describing a surface is to state the value of the $n+1^{th}$ coordinate of the surface as a function of the first n coordinates, or

$$\xi = \phi(x)$$

This is the point description of the surface. There is an alternate means of describing the surface: in terms of its tangent planes. If the surface is strictly concave, then no two points on the surface can have tangent planes with identical normal vectors. Thus the surface may be described by stating for each possible tangent vector the intercept of the corresponding tangent plane with the $n+1^{th}$ axis. Assume the $n+1^{th}$ component of the tangent vector to be always -1, and represent its first n components by the vector y. Then if η is the value of the intercept along the $n+1^{th}$ axis, the tangent plane description is given by stating η as a function of y.

$$\eta = \theta(y)$$

These two descriptions of the surface are illustrated by Fig. 2-6.

Let us consider the relation between these two descriptions. First, recall that the normal vector of the tangent plane at the point $\overline{x}$ is

$$\begin{bmatrix} y \\ -1 \end{bmatrix} = \begin{bmatrix} \partial\phi(\overline{x}) \\ -1 \end{bmatrix}$$

Hence the equation of the tangent plane to the surface at $\overline{x}$ is

$$(x - \overline{x})^T \, \partial\phi(\overline{x}) - [\eta - \phi(\overline{x})] = 0 \tag{2-9}$$

The intercept $\overline{\eta}$ of this plane with the $n+1^{th}$ coordinate axis may be found by setting $x = 0$ in 2-9.

$$\overline{\eta} = \phi(\overline{x}) - \overline{x}^T \, \partial\phi(\overline{x}) \tag{2-10}$$

This expression for $\overline{\eta}$ can be put in terms of y provided that the relation

$$y = \partial\phi(x)$$

can be solved to give x in terms of y.

$$x = \partial\phi^{-1}(y)$$

That this is possible when ϕ is strictly concave is based on the fact that there is a unique tangent plane for each point on the surface (Theorem E-2). Substituting this relation in 2-10, the functional relation for the tangent plane description of the surface is obtained in terms of the functional relation for the point description.

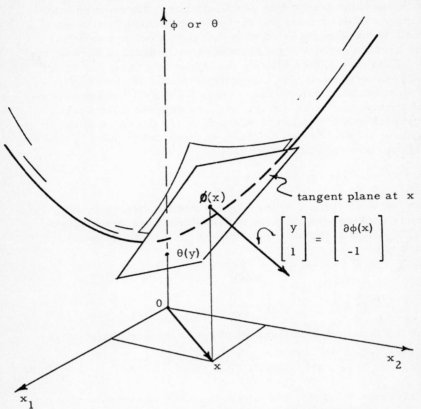

Fig. 2-6 The Legendre transformation

$$\eta = \theta(y) = \phi \left[\partial\phi^{-1}(y) \right] - y^T \left[\partial\phi^{-1}(y) \right] \qquad (2\text{-}11)$$

This function is the <u>Legendre transformation</u> of ϕ and turns out to be strictly convex (Theorems E-1 and E-3) if ϕ is strictly concave.

The development given in Appendix E yields a slight general-ization of the Legendre transformation as presented by Courant and Hilbert [6]. While their formulation requires the initial function to be twice differentiable, the author's development, by utilizing the concavity property, requires only first differ-entiability.

An important property of the Legendre transform is that its gradient is the negative inverse of the gradient of ϕ. Specifically,

$$\partial\theta(y) = -\partial\phi^{-1}(y)$$

This is easily shown by application of the chain rule for differentiating composite functions (see Appendix E).

As an example of the Legendre transformation, consider the case where ϕ is a positive definite quadratic form (and hence a strictly concave function).

$$\phi(x) = \frac{1}{2} x^T P x$$

Then the gradient of ϕ is

$$\partial\phi(x) = P x$$

Since P is positive definite, its inverse exists and is also positive definite. Therefore,

$$\partial\phi^{-1}(y) = P^{-1} y$$

The Legendre transform may now be evaluated using 2-11.

$$\theta(y) = \frac{1}{2} (P^{-1}y)^T P P^{-1} y - [P^{-1}y, y]$$

$$= -\frac{1}{2} y^T P^{-1} y$$

The transform $\theta(y)$ is obviously a strictly convex function. Its gradient is

$$\partial\theta(y) = - P^{-1} y$$

in agreement with the statement made above.

Duality in Equality Constrained Minimization

In order to introduce the discussion of duality relationships in programming problems, a simple problem will be used to illustrate duality in an ordinary equality constrained minimization problem. Consider the problem of minimizing a positive definite quadratic form subject to a system of linear constraints.

Quadratic Minimum Problem:
    Minimize

$$\frac{1}{2} x^T P x + c^T x$$

with

$$A x = b$$

Applying the Lagrange multiplier rule, the following equivalent problem is obtained.

Quadratic Lagrangian Problem:
Find vectors x and z such that

$$A^T z - P x = c$$

$$A x = b$$

Now, as was shown above, the Legendre transform of $\phi(x) = \frac{1}{2} x^T P x$ is $\theta(y) = -\frac{1}{2} y^T P^{-1} y$. Consider a second extremum problem concerning the maximization of the transform:

Quadratic Maximum Problem:
Maximize

$$-\frac{1}{2} y^T P^{-1} y - b^T z$$

with

$$A^T z - y = c$$

The corresponding result of use of the multiplier rule is the following:

Quadratic Lagrangian Problem:
Find an x, y, and z such that

$$A^T z - y = c$$

$$x = P^{-1} y$$

$$A x = b$$

The two Lagrangian problems are identical except for the introduction of the extra variables y in the latter case. This indicates that the two extremum formulations are simply two different but equivalent ways of stating the same problem. The close connection between the two extremum problems is further brought out by the following property.

If x is an optimal vector of the minimum problem and (y, z) is an optimal vector of the maximum problem, then the objective functions are equal.

This is a slightly altered form of an equivalence statement given by Courant and Hilbert [5]. To demonstrate it, let (x, y, z) be a solution of the Lagrangian problem. It follows that x is an optimal solution of the minimization problem and (y, z) is an optimal solution of the maximization problem. The following relations are easily obtained from the Lagrangian problem:

$$c^T x = x^T A^T z - x^T y$$

$$b^T z = z^T A x = x^T A^T z$$

It follows that

$$c^T x - b^T z = - x^T y \tag{2-12}$$

The difference between the objective functions of the two extremum problems is

$$\Delta = \frac{1}{2} x^T P x + c^T x - [-\frac{1}{2} y^T P^{-1} y + b^T z]$$

or, using 2-12

$$\Delta = \frac{1}{2} x^T P x - x^T y + \frac{1}{2} y^T P^{-1} y$$

and finally, using the relation $x = P^{-1} y$,

$$\Delta = \frac{1}{2} x^T y - x^T y + \frac{1}{2} y^T x = 0$$

Thus the objective functions take on the same value for the optimal solution. This principle of equality of objective functions carries over into the duality relations in linear and quadratic programming which are presented in the next section.

Duality in Mathematical Programming

The duality relation established above for a simple quadratic minimum problem can be generalized to a class of quadratic programming problems. Consider the following pair of quadratic programs:

Primal Quadratic Program:
Minimize

$$\frac{1}{2} x_Q^T P x_Q + c_Q^T x_Q + c_L^T x_L$$

with

$$A_Q x_Q + A_L x_L \geq b$$

$$x_Q \geq 0, \quad x_L \geq 0$$

24

Dual Quadratic Program:
 Maximize

$$-\frac{1}{2} y_Q^{\ T} P^{-1} y_Q + b^T y_L$$

with

$$A_Q^{\ T} y_L - y_Q \leq c_Q$$

$$A_L^{\ T} y_L \leq c_L$$

$$y_L \geq 0, \quad y_Q \text{ unrestricted}$$

Each of the objective functions consists of a positive definite quadratic form in one set of variables plus a linear combination of other variables, and the quadratic form in the dual problem is the Legendre transform of the quadratic form in the primal. These two extremum problems have the same generalized Lagrangian problem, namely the following:

Generalized Quadratic Lagrangian Problem:
 Find x, v, u, and y such that

$$A_Q x_Q + A_L x_L - u = b \qquad \text{primal}$$
$$x_Q \geq 0 \quad x_L \geq 0 \quad u \geq 0 \qquad \text{constraints}$$

$$A_Q^{\ T} y_L - y_Q + v_Q = c_Q \qquad \text{dual}$$
$$A_L^{\ T} y_L + v_L = c_L \qquad \text{constraints}$$

$$y_L \geq 0 \quad v_Q \geq 0 \quad v_L \geq 0$$

$$x_Q = P^{-1} y_Q \qquad \text{primal-dual coupling}$$

$$x_Q^{\ T} v_Q = 0$$
$$x_L^{\ T} v_L = 0 \qquad \text{complementary slackness conditions}$$
$$y_L^{\ T} u = 0$$

The important properties of the dual pair of quadratic programs are summarized in three fundamental theorems which are proved in Appendix D.

Duality Theorem: A feasible vector of the primal program is optimal if and only if there is a feasible vector of the dual program such that the primal and dual objective functions are equal. A feasible vector of the dual program is optimal if and only if there is a feasible vector of the primal program for which the objective functions are equal.

Existence Theorem: If both the primal and the dual program possess a feasible vector, then both have optimal vectors. If either of the two programs has no feasible vector, then neither has an optimal vector.

Complementary Slackness Principle: i) If (x_Q, x_L) is an optimal solution of the primal program and (y_Q, y_L) is an optimal solution of the dual program, then (x_Q, x_L, y_Q, y_L) is a solution of the Lagrangian problem. In particular the coupling relation and complementary slackness conditions are satisfied. ii) The values of the variables x_Q and y_Q are unique in optimal solutions of the primal and dual, respectively.

An important point in connection with quadratic programming is that the associated Lagrangian problem consists only of linear relations. This feature allows linear computations to be used in obtaining optimal solutions, and allows finite step algorithms to be designed. This would not be true for any more general class of programming problems.

The pair of quadratic programs stated above becomes the well-known pair of dual linear programs if the matrices P, A_Q, c_Q, x_Q, and y_Q are omitted.

Primal Linear Program:

Minimize $c^T x$

with $A x \geq b$

$x \geq 0$

Dual Linear Program:

Maximize $b^T y$

with $A^T y \leq c$

$y \geq 0$

Thus the duality principle for quadratic program bridges
the gap between the familiar duality relation in linear programming and the equivalence principle stated by Courant and Hilbert
for equality constrained minimization problems. It is an out-
growth of the equivalent problems for quadratic programming
given by Frank and Wolfe [16] and especially Hildreth [17].

Unfortunately the duality principle as stated above is only
applicable to quadratic programs in which the coefficients of
the objective function have the form

$$Q = \begin{bmatrix} P & 0 \\ 0 & 0 \end{bmatrix}$$

where P is positive definite. Dorn [12] has given a dual problem
in which Q may be an arbitrary positive semidefinite matrix. However, Q then appears in the constraint relations of the dual problem
and hence the duality does not have the symmetry of the formulation presented here.

On the other hand, the duality relationship can be extended by
means of the Legendre transformation to yield a pair of dual concave programs. The primal concave program is obtained by replacing the positive definite form of the primal quadratic program
by a concave function $\phi(x_Q)$. The dual convex program is obtained
by substituting the Legendre transform of $\phi(x_Q)$ for the negative
definite form of the dual quadratic program. The pertinent theory
is given in Appendix F.

Fenchel [14] has demonstrated the following very general duality
principle: Given a concave function ϕ defined on an arbitrary convex set C, there is (subject to slight qualification) a convex set
D and a convex function θ defined on D such that ϕ takes on a
minimum over C if and only if θ takes on a maximum over D, and
these two extrema are the same. The rules given for the construction of D and θ when C and ϕ are given make this the ultimate
generalization of the Legendre transformation. In theory at least,
this is a duality principle applicable to the general programming
problem. However, it is expressed only in terms of a general
notion of convex sets. In order to apply the principle to practical
problems it would be desirable to know, given the objective and
constraint functions of a general programming problem, how to
construct the objective function of the dual problem and the convex
functions defining the dual constraint set. The duality principle for
quadratic and concave programs answers this question for the
linear constraints case, but it has not been resolved for the
general programming problem.

Chapter 3

PROPERTIES AND EQUIVALENT FORMULATIONS
FOR ELECTRICAL NETWORKS CONTAINING DIODES

It has long been known that there are several equivalent formulations for the problem of solving a network of resistors and
sources. Maxwell noted in 1873 [24] that the current distribution
in a network of resistors and current sources which produced the
least "heating" was the one which satisfied the Kirchoff loop condition. The present author, though, knows of no place in the literature where extremum formulations for electrical networks
containing diodes are discussed. Investigations of these networks
have been based on the Kirchoff laws and the properties of the
diode. Actually their behavior is precisely described by the optimal vectors of corresponding mathematical programs. This inti-
mate connection between electrical circuit theory and mathematical programming is the subject of this chapter.

First the incidence matrix is introduced as a convenient way of
expressing the topology of a network. Then the conditions for the
solution of electrical networks are briefly reviewed, and the characteristics of the idealized electrical devices which will concern us
are defined. With the formal demonstration of the equivalence of
mathematical programming and the solution of certain electrical
networks, physical interpretation of some of the main theoretical
ideas of programming theory are given. Finally, the concepts of
terminal-pair systems and breakpoint curves, which are the basis
for later developments, are introduced.

Graphs and Incidence Matrices

A graph is a set of points which are called nodes connected by a
set of line segments known as branches. Each branch of the graph
connects two distinct nodes and has an associated direction indicated
by an arrowhead. A graph is illustrated in Fig. 3-1a. We will be
concerned with only connected graphs in which any node is connected
to each other node by some sequence of branches of the graph. Gen-
erally when one is using the concept of a graph, it is only the topology of the graph that is important, that is, the description of
which node pair is connected by each branch. This information
may be conveniently given in a rectangular array having one row
for each node and one column for each branch of the graph. In each
column of the array a -1 is placed in the row corresponding to the

27

a)

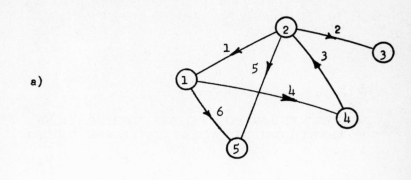

branches

		1	2	3	4	5	6
	1	1			-1		1
	2	-1	-1	1		-1	
nodes	3		1				
	4			-1	1		
	5					1	-1

b)

Fig. 3-1 A graph and its incidence matrix

node on which the branch originates; a +1 is placed in the row corresponding to the node on which the branch terminates. The remaining positions in the column are 0 . The array so constructed is called the node-incidence matrix of the graph. An example is given in Fig. 3-1b for the graph in Fig. 3-1a. The node-incidence matrix description of a graph will be used in all mathematical formulations developed in this chapter. An alternate topological description may be obtained by listing the incidence of branches on loops and leads to a dual network development. This description will not be used in the present work.

Electrical Networks: Laws and Devices

An electrical network is a graph in which various electrical devices are associated with the branches. With each branch i of the graph is associated a voltage e_i and a current i_i . The sense chosen for these variables is indicated in Fig. 3-2. It is such that

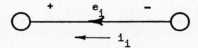

Fig. 3-2 Branch polarity convention

the product $e_i i_i$ is the <u>power delivered</u> to the network by the branch. With each node j is associated a <u>node potential</u> u_j . In order that a given set of values of e_i, i_i , and u_j be a <u>solu</u>-<u>tion of the</u> network, it is necessary and sufficient that three conditions be satisfied. They are:

1) [Kirchoff's node law] The branch currents must satisfy a continuity condition at the nodes.

$$\sum_i i_i - \sum_k i_k = 0$$

i covers all branches directed toward node j .
k covers all branches directed away from node j .

Using the node-incidence matrix N this may be written as

$$N \ i \ = \ 0$$

where i is the column matrix of branch currents.

2) [Kirchoff's loop law] The difference between potentials of the nodes on which a branch is incident must equal the branch voltage. This requires

$$u_j - u_i = e_k$$

if branch k is directed from node i to node j . This may be written, using the node-incidence matrix, as

$$N^T u = e$$

in which u and e are the column matrices of node potentials and voltages, respectively. This condition is clearly equivalent to the requirement that the sum of the branch voltages around any loop equal zero.

3) The current-voltage pair for each branch must satisfy any conditions imposed by the electrical device associated with that branch of the graph.

There are five different types of electrical devices that will be considered in this chapter. Their symbols and the conditions which they impose on the voltage-current pair for each branch are shown in Fig. 3-3. The <u>current source</u> maintains a constant branch current regardless of what may happen to the branch voltage. Similarly the <u>voltage source</u> maintains a constant branch voltage. The

30

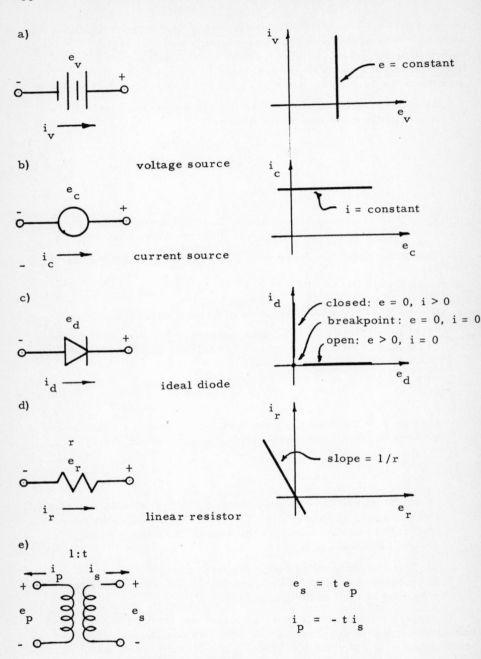

a)

e_v

i_v

voltage source

e = constant

b)

e_c

i_c

current source

i = constant

c)

e_d

i_d

ideal diode

closed: e = 0, i > 0
breakpoint: e = 0, i = 0
open: e > 0, i = 0

d)

r

e_r

i_r

linear resistor

slope = 1/r

e)

1 : t

i_p i_s

e_p e_s

$$e_s = t \, e_p$$

$$i_p = -t \, i_s$$

ideal d-c transformer

Fig. 3-3 Relations imposed by electrical
branch types

diode acts like a switch. It maintains zero voltage as long as the current is greater than zero, and zero current if the voltage is greater than zero. The diode requirements may be stated concisely as

$$e_d \geq 0, \quad i_d \geq 0, \quad e_d i_d = 0$$

The last of these relations states that a diode always delivers zero power to the network. A diode will be considered as having three mutually exclusive states:

open $\quad\quad e_d > 0, \quad i_d = 0$

breakpoint $e_d = 0, \quad i_d = 0$

closed $\quad\quad e_d = 0, \quad i_d > 0$

The resistor imposes a linear relation between branch current and voltage. The power delivered by the resistor is

$$e_r i_r = - \frac{e_r^2}{r} = - i_r^2 r$$

which is a quadratic function of the branch voltage or current. The ideal d-c transformer is a device associated with two branches of the graph of a network. One branch is associated with the primary winding of the transformer and has current i_p and voltage e_p. The other branch is associated with the secondary winding with current i_s and voltage e_s. From the conditions imposed by the transformer,

$$e_s = t e_p, \quad i_p = - t i_s$$

it follows that

$$e_p i_p = - e_s i_s$$

that is, a transformer delivers zero power to a network, although it may transfer it from one branch to another.

Equivalent Problems for Diode-Source-Resistor Networks

In this section electrical networks containing voltage sources, current sources, diodes, and resistors will be considered. The vectors e and i representing the branch voltages and currents will be partitioned according to type of branch (by renumbering the branches if necessary).

$$e = \begin{bmatrix} e_V \\ e_C \\ e_D \\ e_R \end{bmatrix} \qquad i = \begin{bmatrix} i_V \\ i_C \\ i_D \\ i_R \end{bmatrix}$$

The columns of the node-incidence matrix will be similarly partitioned so that

$$N = [\, N_V \ N_C \ N_D \ N_R \,]$$

The network laws as applied to a diode-source-resistor network may now be written down.

Diode-Source-Resistor Lagrangian Problem

Find e, i, and u such that

$$N_V i_V + N_D i_D + N_R i_R = -N_C i_C \qquad \text{Kirchoff node law}$$

$$\left.\begin{aligned}
N_V{}^T u &= e_V \\
N_D{}^T u - e_D &= 0 \\
N_R{}^T u - e_R &= 0 \\
N_C{}^T u - e_C &= 0
\end{aligned}\right\} \qquad \text{Kirchoff loop law}$$

$$e_R + R\, i_R = 0 \qquad \text{Resistor requirements}$$

$$e_D \geq 0, \quad i_D \geq 0, \quad e_D{}^T i_D = 0 \qquad \text{Diode requirements}$$

Here R is the diagonal matrix of resistance values. The terms $N_C i_C$ and e_V have been put on the right as they are given constants representing the conditions imposed by the sources. The significant point is that this set of relations is precisely the Lagrangian problem associated with the following pair of dual quadratic programs.

Diode-Source-Resistor Primal Problem:

Find an i that minimizes

$$\frac{1}{2} i_R^T R i_R - e_V^T i_V$$

subject to

$$N_V i_V + N_D i_D + N_R i_R = -N_C i_C$$

$$i_D \geq 0$$

Diode-Source-Resistor Dual Problem:

Find an e and a u that maximizes

$$-\frac{1}{2} e_R^T G e_R + i_C^T e_C$$

subject to

$$N_V^T u = e_V$$

$$N_D^T u - e_D = 0$$

$$N_R^T u - e_R = 0$$

$$N_C^T u - e_C = 0$$

$$e_D \geq 0$$

In the dual problem, $G = R^{-1}$ is the diagonal matrix of the conductance values for the resistance branches. In the primal formulation the variables are branch currents, and the node potentials are the Lagrange multipliers. Conversely, the dual problem concerns voltage quantities, and the branch currents are the Lagrange multipliers. The coupling relation of the Lagrangian problem is a consequence of the resistor requirements. Therefore, if the network contains no resistors, the coupling relation disappears and the problem statements reduce to a pair of dual linear programs. The above two problems have the following corresponding statements in words:

Primal: Find a feasible current distribution in the network which minimizes the sum of the power absorbed by the voltage sources and one half the power absorbed by the resistors.

Dual: Find a feasible voltage distribution in the network which maximizes the power delivered to the network by the current sources minus one half the power absorbed by the resistors.

If there are no diodes or voltage sources in the network, the above primal problem becomes the well-known rule that the solution of a source-resistor network is that particular current distribution, among all current distributions satisfying Kirchoff's node law, which minimizes the power dissipated in the resistors. With voltage sources but still no diodes, the primal statement is the more general rule given by Maxwell.

This correspondence between programming problems and electrical network problems yields some very nice physical interpretations of the mathematical principles of programming:

1) The inequality constraints in the programming problem are embodied in the diode requirements in the electrical network.

2) The complementary slackness principle corresponds to the requirement that diodes deliver zero power to an electrical network.

3) The duality theorem states that the objective functions in the primal and dual formulations are equal at the solution point. In the electrical network problem this requires

$$e_V^T i_V - \frac{1}{2} i_R^T R i_R - \frac{1}{2} e_R^T G e_R + e_C^T i_C = 0$$

which is clearly a statement of the principle of conservation of energy.

Reduced Networks

An interpretation of the existence theorem of mathematical programming can be given in terms of the reduced networks associated with a given source-diode-resistor network.

The voltage-reduced network associated with a given diode-source resistor network is obtained by replacing each resistor or current source of the original network with an open circuit.

The current-reduced network associated with a given diode-source resistor network is obtained by replacing each resistor or voltage source of the original network with a short circuit.

The equations for the voltage-reduced network are obtained by setting i_C equal to zero and replacing the resistor conditions with $i_R = 0$ in the Lagrangian problem. It is evident by inspection that if (i, e, u) is a solution of the voltage-reduced network, then i satisfies the constraints of the primal programming formulation. Conversely, if i satisfies the primal constraints, then (i, e = 0, u = 0) is evidently a solution of the voltage-reduced network. Therefore the primal constraints are feasible if and only if the voltage-reduced network has a solution. Similarly, the equations for the current-reduced network are obtained by setting e_V equal to zero and replacing the resistor conditions with $e_R = 0$ in the Lagrangian problem. As above, one concludes that the constraints of the dual programming formulation are feasible if and only if the current-reduced network possesses a solution. The existence theorem of quadratic (or linear) programming (Theorem D-3) then has the following physical statement in terms of electrical networks.

> An electrical network made up of sources, diodes, and resistors possesses a solution if and only if the associated voltage-reduced and current-reduced networks both possess solutions.

The fact that the voltage-reduced network has a solution apparently guarantees that none of the voltage sources are "shorted out" in the original network. The fact that the current-reduced network has a solution guarantees that all the current produced by the current sources has a "place to go."

The correspondence between network problems and programming problems also yields nice physical interpretations of algorithms for solving linear and quadratic programs as will be seen in the following chapters.

Electrical Networks Containing Transformers

The general case of a network made up of voltage sources, current sources, diodes, resistors, and ideal d-c transformers will be considered next. In this case the current vector i will be partitioned to include also i_P and i_S, the primary and secondary transformer currents. The branch voltage vector e will also contain e_P and e_S, the primary and secondary transformer voltages. The incidence matrix is expanded to include N_P and N_S giving the incidence of transformer primary and secondary windings on nodes. The diagonal matrix T gives the turns ratios of the transformers. Expressing the network laws in these terms gives the following set of relations:

Transformer Network Lagrangian Problem:

Find e , i , and u such that

$$N_V \, i_V + N_D \, i_D + N_R \, i_R + N_P i_P + N_S \, i_S = - N_C \, i_C$$

Kirchoff node law

$$N_V^T \, u = e_V$$

$$N_D^T \, u - e_D = 0$$

$$N_R^T \, u - e_R = 0$$

$$N_P^T \, u - e_P = 0$$

$$N_S^T \, u - e_S = 0$$

Kirchoff loop law

$$e_R + R \, i_R = 0 \qquad \text{resistor conditions}$$

$$e_S - T \, e_P = 0, \quad i_P + T \, i_S = 0 \qquad \text{transformer conditions}$$

$$e_D \geq 0, \quad i_D \geq 0, \quad e_D^T \, i_D = 0 \qquad \text{diode conditions}$$

This is the Lagrangian problem corresponding to the following pair of dual quadratic programs.

<u>Transformer Network Primal Problem:</u>

Find an i that minimizes

$$\frac{1}{2} i_R^T \, R \, i_R - e_V^T \, i_V$$

subject to

$$N_V \, i_V + N_D \, i_D + N_R \, i_R + N_P \, i_P + N_S \, i_S = - N_C \, i_C$$

$$i_P + T \, i_S = 0$$

$$i_D \geq 0$$

Transformer Network Dual Problem:

Find an e and a u that maximizes

$$-\frac{1}{2} e_R^T G e_R + i_C^T e_C$$

subject to

$$N_V^T u = e_V$$

$$N_D^T u - e_D$$

$$N_R^T u - e_R = 0$$

$$N_P^T u - e_P = 0$$

$$N_S^T u - e_S = 0$$

$$e_S - T e_P = 0$$

$$e_D \geq 0$$

Thus every electrical network containing the five types of devices treated here is equivalent to a pair of dual quadratic programs. It will be shown later (in Chapter 6) that the reverse is also true: every quadratic (or linear) program can be represented by an electrical network containing only these five types of elements. All of the remarks made above concerning the physical interpretation of the principles of mathematical programming apply without modification when transformers are included.

The important point of difference between networks without transformers and networks with transformers is the following: In the former, the coefficients in the constraint relations of the primal and dual formulations are all either +1 , -1 , or 0 . Indeed, they are the elements of an incidence matrix. In linear programming this fact allows algorithms to be devised in which the arithmetic involves only additions and subtractions. The importance of this will be seen in the next chapter where such an algorithm is developed. With transformers included, the turns ratio matrix T appears in the constraint relations and the coefficients therefore need not even be integers.

Nonlinear Devices

The correspondence between programming problems and network problems can be carried even one step further. In place of the linear resistors included in the networks discussed above, a general class of nonlinear resistors will be allowed. The voltage-current relation of the device will be required to be a "strictly decreasing" curve. Precisely, if (i_r, e_r) and $(\bar{i}_r, \bar{e}_r)$ are any two points on the curve, then

$$i_r < \bar{i}_r \quad \text{if and only if} \quad e_r > \bar{e}_r$$

Otherwise the curve is arbitrary. The characteristics of such a device are illustrated in Fig. 3-4. Obviously the linear resistor is a special case of this device. For this class of devices the relation between current and voltage is one-to-one.

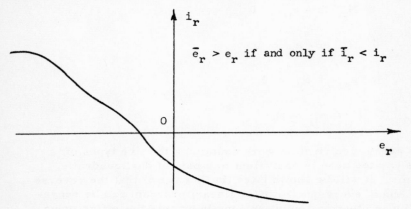

$\bar{e}_r > e_r$ if and only if $\bar{i}_r < i_r$

Fig. 3-4 Nonlinear resistive device

For a network containing voltage and current sources, diodes, transformers, and the general resistive devices, the Lagrangian problem is the same as for the transformer network above except that the nonlinear resistors are described by a relation

$$e_R = f(i_R)$$

where f is a one-to-one transformation. As a result we may also write

$$i_R = f^{-1}(e_R) = -g(e_R)$$

From the properties of convex functions (Appendix E), one concludes that f is the differential of some concave function ϕ and g is the differential of some convex function θ. The net result is that the solution of a network of this type is equivalent to a pair of dual concave programming problems which are identical to the quadratic programs stated above, except that the quadratic forms are replaced by $\phi(i_R)$ in the primal formulation and by $\theta(e_R)$ in the dual formulation.

Terminal Solutions and Breakpoint Curves

The concepts of terminal solutions and breakpoint curve are of utmost importance in the algorithms which will be described in succeeding chapters. For this reason these ideas will be introduced here.

Consider an arbitrary network containing sources, diodes, resistors, and transformers in which one pair of nodes (the terminal pair) is available for external observation (see Fig. 3-5). The current and voltage at the terminal pair will be represented by δ and ϵ, respectively. The nodes which comprise the terminal pair will be indicated by the one

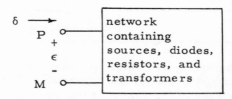

Fig. 3-5 Network with observable terminal pair

column incidence matrix n_T which contains -1 in the position corresponding to node M and +1 in the position corresponding to node P. By a terminal solution is meant a pair of values of δ and ϵ which corresponds to some solution of the network. Terminal-pair solutions thus correspond to solutions of the terminal-pair system of relations given below.

Terminal-Pair System

$$N i + n_T \delta = 0 \qquad \text{Kirchoff node law}$$

$$\left.\begin{array}{l} N^T u = e \\[4pt] n_T^{\,T} u = - \epsilon \end{array}\right\} \qquad \text{Kirchoff loop law}$$

$$e_R = - R i_R \qquad \text{resistor conditions}$$

$$e_S = T e_P, \quad i_P = - T i_S \qquad \text{transformer conditions}$$

$$i_D \geq 0, \quad e_D \geq 0, \quad e_D^{\,T} i_D = 0 \qquad \text{diode conditions}$$

This system of relations may also be set down in tabular form as follows:

ε	i_R	i_V	i_D	i_P	i_S	δ	u	e_P	e_D	
	N_R	N_V	N_D	N_P	N_S	n_T				$-N_C i_C$
				-I	-T					0
	-R						N_R^T			0
							N_V^T			e_V
							N_D^T		I	0
							N_P^T	-I		0
1							N_S^T	-T		0
							n_T^T			0

The line joining the vector variables i_D and e_D indicates that these variables are required to satisfy the "diode conditions." The system above is a special case of the general terminal-pair system

η	x	ξ	y	v	
	A	e			b
	-Q		A^T	I	c
1			e^T		0

An electrical model for this mathematical system will be given in Chapter 5.

A breakpoint curve is a continuous curve made up of straight line segments, none of which has negative slope. An example is given in Fig. 3-6. In Appendix G it is demonstrated that the set of values of

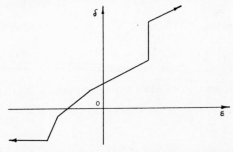

Fig. 3-6 An example of a breakpoint curve

(ξ, η), which correspond to solutions of the general terminal-pair system, form a breakpoint curve in the ξ-η plane. In the following an attempt will be made to make this plausible by means of physical arguments relating to electrical networks. For this purpose it is helpful to view the network as in Fig. 3-7, separating the diodes from the network by placing each one at its own terminal pair. For any solution of the terminal-pair system, each diode either is "open,"

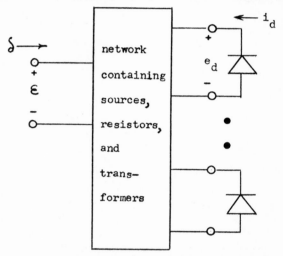

Fig. 3-7 Network with diodes separated

has zero current, and behaves as an open circuit, or is "closed," has zero voltage, and behaves as a short circuit (disregarding the breakpoint state for the present). For a given state of each diode (open or closed) it is clear physically that, since the network contains only linear devices, there will be a unique incremental resistance observed at the terminal pair. This incremental resistance may be zero, or it might be an open circuit, but it can never be negative. Suppose there is more than one terminal solution of the system for a given state of the diodes. Then all points on the line joining these two solutions must also be terminal solutions, because the system is a set of linear equations for any given configuration of diode states. The slope of the line segment must be equal to the incremental resistance. Since there are only a finite number of possible choices of diode states, the set of terminal solutions must consist of a finite number of straight line segments.

Now consider connecting a variable voltage source and one-ohm resistor to the terminal pair, as shown in Fig. 3-8, and suppose that the voltage has been adjusted so that the network has a solution. As the variable voltage α is raised, the terminal solution will move along the line segment corresponding to the present state of the diodes. At some point a diode current or voltage will reach zero and that diode

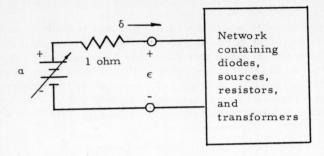

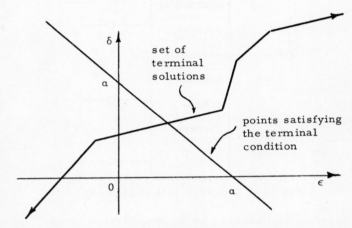

Fig. 3-8 Demonstrating the continuity of the set of
terminal solutions

will shift from the open state, through the breakpoint state to the
closed state, and the terminal solution will be on a new line segment. As the variable voltage is further increased, the states of the
diodes will change, generating the successive line segments of the
breakpoint curve. Eventually, since there are only a finite number
of combinations of diode states, a state will be reached where no
amount of inecrease in the voltage α will cause any diode to shift
to a new state. Thus the last segment of the breakpoint curve must
extend indefinitely toward positive terminal voltage and current. The
same arguments apply regarding the negative portion of the set of
terminal solutions. This is a physical description of the mathematical technique used to prove the corresponding properties of the general
terminal-pair system in a rigorous manner in Appendix G.

A couple of special cases of the terminal-pair system are sufficiently
important to be worth special comment. First, if the network contains
no resistors, the incremental resistance observed at the terminal pair

must always be either zero or an open circuit. Hence the breakpoint curve would contain only horizontal and vertical line segments. Moreover, if the voltage sources of the network are set to zero or removed, all horizontal line segments must be coincident with the current axis. This is true because the vertical positions of such line segments are determined by the voltage sources. Similarly, all vertical line segments of the breakpoint curve collapse to the voltage axis if all current sources are set to zero. These results are demonstrated for the general terminal-pair system as Theorems G-2 and G-3.

Chapter 4

AN ALGORITHM FOR SOLVING ELECTRICAL
MODELS OF NETWORK FLOW PROBLEMS

An important and interesting special class of mathematical programming problems concerns the flow of some conceptual quantity
in a network. The network may be depicted as a set of nodes inter-
connected by branches as shown in Fig. 4-1. The quantity supposed
to be flowing in the network could be almost anything - consumer
goods through a distribution system, communications messages in

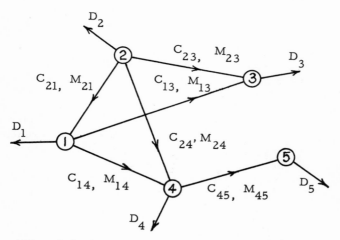

Fig. 4-1 A network flow problem

a transmission system, or automobile traffic through a highway network, for example. For the problems considered in this chapter the
flow quantity must satisfy an important assumption: The flow must
be conserved at the nodes of the network. This means that the total
flow into a node of the network must always equal the total flow out:

$$\sum_j X_{ij} = \sum_j X_{ji} + D_i \qquad (4-1)$$

where D_i is the amount of flow (positive, negative, or zero) required
to enter the network at node i . For each branch of the network two
parameters may be specified giving the character of the branch. The
first is a unit cost C_{ij} for flow in the branch directed from node i
to node j . The second parameter is the capacity M_{ij} of a branch

45

which places an upper limit on the amount of flow X_{ij} permitted in the branch.

$$X_{ij} \leq M_{ij} \tag{4-2}$$

The optimal flow problem is to determine the pattern of flow which gives the lowest total cost while satisfying the continuity conditions and capacity restrictions.

Minimize $\sum_{i,j} C_{ij} X_{ij}$

with $\sum_{j} X_{ij} - \sum_{j} X_{ji} = D_i \tag{4-3}$

and $0 \leq X_{ij} \leq M_{ij}$

Problems of this type are clearly linear mathematical programs. A wide variety of allocation, distribution, and assignment problems are encompassed by the network flow model. For example, the well-known transportation problem [18] can easily be interpreted in terms of flow in a network.

A type of flow not usually discussed in connection with network flow problems is the flow of current in electric circuits. There is, however, an elegant and useful analogy here which forms the basis of this chapter. In succeeding paragraphs electric network models are constructed for two special cases of network flow problems. In the first, only capacity parameters are assigned to the branches, and in the second, the branches are described by cost values alone. Then a model is constructed for the general network flow problem 4-3, in which both costs and capacity restrictions are allowed. Each of these electrical models consists entirely of current sources, voltage sources, and ideal diodes. It follows that a procedure which can produce a solution for an arbitrary network of diodes and sources is also capable of finding the optimal flow pattern for any network flow problem. Such an algorithm constitutes the principal contribution of this chapter. The algorithm is stated in the language of electric circuit analysis, because this language makes possible a very neat and concise presentation and yields considerable intuitive knowledge of the procedure.

The method to be described is similar in nature to the Ford-Fulkerson procedure for solving the transportation problem [15]. These authors have indicated the extension of their method to the general network flow problem, and the details of the extension are given by Jewell [19]. The algorithm described here, however, is somewhat more general and considerably more flexible, and has the advantage that successive solutions for the same network, but with modified parameter values, may be computed by starting from any previous solution of the network.

At the end of the chapter the connection between the author's algorithm and related methods for solving network flow problems is given.

The Maximum Flow Problem

As the first special case of the general network flow problem, consider a network in which a branch directed from node i to node j is assigned an upper limit M_{ij} and a lower limit $-M_{ji}$ on the flow X_{ij} in the branch, so that

$$-M_{ji} \leq X_{ij} \leq M_{ij}$$

Such a network is shown in Fig. 4-2. It is desired to determine the maximum flow which may enter the network at node a and subsequently leave at node b . From this we may form a problem which agrees in

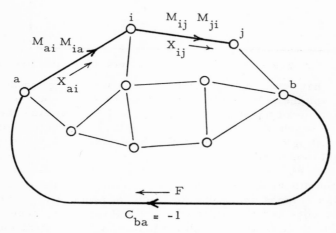

Fig. 4-2 The maximum flow problem

statement with the general network flow formulation 4-3 by introducing a unit cost branch as shown in Fig. 4-2. Then the total cost for a flow distribution in the network is -F , and the minimum cost distribution is clearly also the one which maximizes the flow from a to b . The mathematical statement of the maximum flow problem is then

Maximize   F

with

$$\sum_j X_{ij} - \sum_j X_{ji} = \begin{cases} F, & i = a \\ -F, & i = b \\ 0, & i \neq a, b \end{cases} \tag{4-4}$$

$$-M_{ji} \leq X_{ij} \leq M_{ij} \tag{4-5}$$

With the aid of the results of Chapter 3 we may synthesize an electrical model (Fig. 4-3) for this linear program. Each branch of the

48

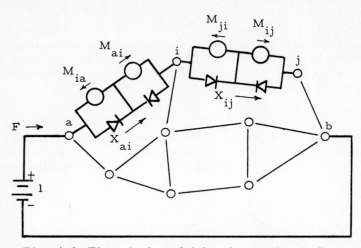

Fig. 4-3 Electrical model for the maximum flow problem

flow network has been replaced by a combination of current sources
and diodes, and the unit cost branch by a unit voltage source. Since
the electrical model has more nodes than the flow network, the nodes
of the former which correspond to nodes in the latter will be distinguished by calling them major nodes. The extra nodes introduced in
the electrical model will be called minor nodes. From Chapter 3
(pp. 31-34) we see that a current and voltage distribution which is a
solution of the model will automatically minimize the power absorbed
by the voltage sources under the conditions of nonnegative current
through the diodes and continuity of current flow at each node. Let
X_{ij} represent the current through the diode-current source combination connecting node i to node j, and let F be the current through
the voltage source. Then the continuity condition for current flow
at the major nodes is exactly 4-4. The continuity conditions at the
minor nodes plus the diode requirements yield

$$M_{ij} - X_{ij} \geq 0$$

$$M_{ji} + X_{ij} \geq 0$$

which is equivalent to 4-5. Since the minimization of power absorbed
by the voltage source means maximization of F, the problem of solving the electrical model is mathematically equivalent to the maximum
flow problem. Any selection of currents and voltages which satisfies
the model will indicate the maximum possible flow in the original
network.

Thus the movement of current in the electrical network corresponds
directly to flow in the network of capacitated flow branches. Diodes
in the model place limits on the flow of current corresponding to the

capacity restrictions. The single voltage source forces current through the model to its full capacity and therefore achieves the maximum flow.

The Shortest Path Problem

Next consider a network as shown in Fig. 4-4 in which there are two cost parameters associated with each branch. C_{ij} gives the unit cost for flow X_{ij} directed from node i toward node j, and C_{ji} is the unit cost for flow X_{ji} in the reverse direction. It is desired to determine a routing for one unit of flow from node a to

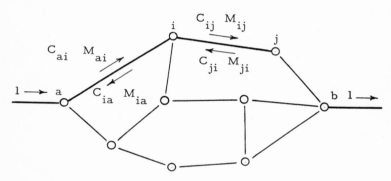

Fig. 4-4 The shortest path problem

node b so that the total cost is minimized. If the cost parameters are interpreted as distances in a highway network, this is equivalent to determining the shortest path from a to b. In mathematical form the problem is

$$\text{Minimize} \quad \sum_{i,j} C_{ij} X_{ij}$$

$$\text{with} \quad \sum_{j} X_{ij} - \sum_{j} X_{ji} = \begin{cases} 1, & i = a \\ -1, & i = b \\ 0, & i \neq a, b \end{cases} \quad (4\text{-}6)$$

$$X_{ij} \geq 0 \quad (4\text{-}7)$$

As in the case of the maximum flow problem, an equivalent electrical network can be set up as shown in Fig. 4-5. This time each flow branch becomes a combination of voltage sources and diodes,

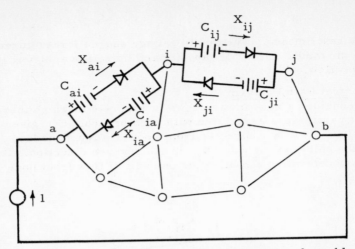

Fig. 4-5 Electrical model of the shortest path problem

and a unit current source forces a unit of current to flow. Again utilizing the results of Chapter 3 (pp. 31-34), it is seen that the continuity condition for the major nodes of the electrical model yields precisely 4-6. The requirement of nonnegative diode currents gives 4-7. Since a solution of the electrical model inherently minimizes

$$\sum_{i,j} C_{ij} X_{ij}$$

or the power absorbed by the voltage sources subject to these restrictions, the branches through which the unit current flows defines the least-cost path through the network.

Thus the values of the voltage sources correspond to unit costs or prices. This relation may be clarified by considering the dual of the above linear programming problem.

$$\text{Maximize} \quad U_a - U_b$$

$$\text{with} \quad U_i - U_j \leq C_{ij}$$

In terms of the electrical network the U's are to be interpreted as the electric potentials on the nodes. The problem statement requires that the power delivered by the current source be maximized for some set of node potentials which yields nonnegative diode voltages. The potentials U_i also have significance with respect to the flow network: Any solution of the electrical network must satisfy the diode conditions (complementary slackness)

$$[C_{ij} - (U_i - U_j)] \ X_{ij} = 0$$

This requires that the potential difference between any pair of major nodes must equal the unit cost for the branch joining them if there is flow in that branch. Now consider a path from node a to node b in which flow has been established. It follows from the above conclusion that the potential difference $U_a - U_b$ must be exactly the sum of the unit costs for the separate branches of the path. If we take U_b to be zero, then the potential of node a in the electrical model gives directly the cost per unit flow for the shortest path through the network.

The reader may have noticed that the electrical branch for the shortest path problem is precisely the electrical dual of the branch for the maximum flow problem. This duality principle (which is distinct from the duality of mathematical programming) states that in a diode-source network whose graph is planar, if

current sources voltage sources parallel connection series connection	are replaced by	voltage sources current sources series connection parallel connection

then a second electrical network is obtained which obeys precisely the same mathematical relations as the first. In particular the application of the transformation to the electrical model of the maximum flow problem produces the electrical model of a shortest path problem and vice versa.

The General Flow Problem

In the preceding sections we have noted that the following equivalences hold: A voltage source connected in series with a diode is analogous to a unidirectional flow branch with a cost per unit flow equal to the value of the source and an unlimited capacity for flow. A current source in parallel with a diode represents a flow branch with zero unit cost and an upper limit on the amount of flow equal to the value of the source.

The obvious generalization is shown in Fig. 4-6. Combining the two forms yields an electrical branch which incorporates both the unit cost

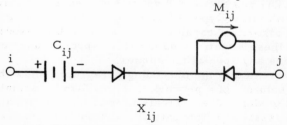

Fig. 4-6 Electrical model of general flow branch

and a capacity limitation. Here for simplicity a unidirectional branch has been drawn, but a bidirectional branch could be obtained by placing two of these in parallel. An electrical model of the general network flow problem illustrated in Fig. 4-1 is formed by replacing the flow branches by electrical branches of this type. Fig. 4-7 shows the model

52

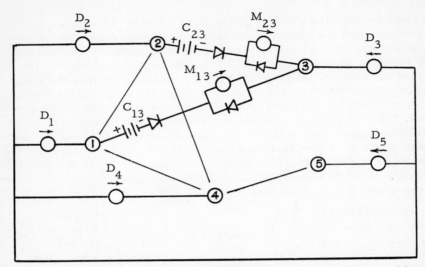

Fig. 4-7 Electrical model of the network flow problem

in which current sources supply the specified flow into the network
at each node. It is readily verified that, as above, any solution of
the network gives an optimal or least-cost distribution for the network flow problem.

A number of variations of this problem may also be modelled by
diode-source networks. For instance the "boundary conditions" on
the network of Fig. 4-1 consist of specification of the amount of
flow that must be absorbed or delivered by the network at each node.
An alternative type of boundary condition might be a source which
could supply or absorb as much flow as desired, but at a fixed price.
The cost of flow to or from such a source is added to the objective
function to be minimized. In the electrical model, a fixed price
source is represented by a voltage source of value equal to the fixed
price. Prager [26] has discussed special procedures for solving
flow problems with either type of boundary condition or a mixture of
the two. For an algorithm capable of solving any diode-source network, however, these situations do not form special cases and therefore do not require any special techniques.

The models presented in the preceding paragraphs show that one
could obtain the solution of a network flow problem by actually setting
up the electrical model. The currents in the model would automatically take on the least-cost flow pattern, and the optimal distribution
of flow for the original network would be obtained by simply measuring the corresponding currents in the model.

Two factors make this an impractical procedure in most cases.
Very efficient digital-computer programs have been devised for solving these problems, and these programs can accept data and produce
results in forms convenient for the user. With the electrical model

the setup and read-out operations would be uneconomically time-consuming, and mechanization of these processes would not be justifiable in view of the availability of digital machines. The second factor concerns the availability of sufficiently precise electrical components. Although reasonably good voltage sources (batteries) and diodes are readily available, current sources of comparable precision and cost are virtually nonexistent. Even the quality of available diodes and batteries are such as to preclude modelling an even moderately large network (about 100-branch) flow problem successfully.

In the particular case of the shortest distance problem, the model contains only a single current source which need not be very precise. Hence solving relatively small problems of this type could well be practical with a diode-source model [2].

Of course the aim of the author in studying these models has been to develop physical insight into the mathematics of the problems and to use them as a guide in formulating the methods presented below.

Existence Conditions and Reduced Networks

Before stating the steps of the computational algorithm, the significance of the existence theorem of mathematical programming must be reviewed in relation to the actual structure of the network. To facilitate the discussion the terms path, loop, and tree will be used to describe certain groups of branches in the graph of a network. Their definitions are:

Path between node i and node j : a sequence of branches and nodes in the graph starting with node i and terminating with node j .

Loop: a path which starts and terminates on the same node.

Tree: a set of branches and nodes of the graph which contains a path between each pair of nodes in the set, but contains no loops.

Full tree: a tree which contains every node of the graph.

It will be supposed that certain redundant branches have been removed from any network considered. Specifically, the following assumptions will be made.

First nonredundancy assumption:
The nodes of the network cannot be divided into two groups such that the only branches connecting members of the two groups are current sources.

In particular, this means that no single node of the network may have current sources only incident on it. If this assumption were not valid, then either the values of these current sources would not add up to zero and the network would possess no solution, or the values of the current sources would cancel and the two sections of the network could be solved separately (See Fig. 4-8).

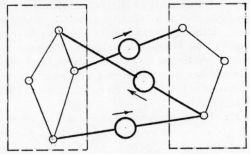

Fig. 4-8 Network violating the first nonredundancy assumption

Second nonredundancy assumption
The network has no loop on which only voltage sources are incident.

If this assumption were not valid, one of the voltage sources could be removed without affecting solutions except for an arbitrary current in the loop (See Fig. 4-9).

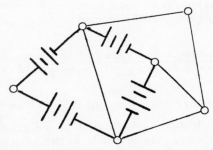

Fig. 4-9 Network violating the second nonredundancy assumption

The following statement gives a necessary and sufficient condition for the existence of solutions for an electrical network constructed of voltage and current sources, ideal diodes, and resistors.

An electrical network whose branches are voltage and current sources, diodes, and resistors possesses a solution if and only if the following two conditions are both satisfied.

First Existence Condition: For each loop of the network on which only diodes and voltage sources are incident and all diodes are aligned in the same way with the loop, the sum of values of the voltage sources aligned with the diodes must not be greater than the sum of values of voltage sources aligned against the diodes.

<u>Second Existence Condition</u>: Divide the nodes into two groups in any manner. For any such division in which all branches connecting nodes of both groups are diodes and current sources and all diodes are directed towards the same group of nodes, the sum of values of the current sources directed toward this group must not exceed the sum of values of the current sources directed away.

These conditions are simply a restatement of the interpretation of the existence theorem of quadratic programming given in the section on reduced networks in Chapter 3. The necessity of these conditions is readily apparent. If the first condition were violated for some loop, then no assignment of potentials to the nodes of the loop could satisfy the branches of the loop. If the second condition were violated for some division of nodes, then no permissible assignment of currents to the diodes could produce a net current between the two groups of nodes equal to zero. (For examples see Figs. 4-10 and 4-11.)

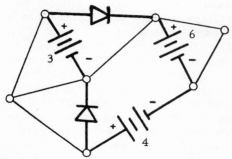

Fig. 4-10 Network violating the first existence condition

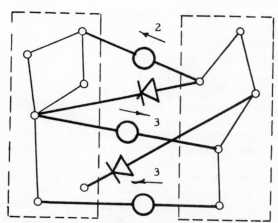

Fig. 4-11 Network violating the second existence condition

The sufficiency of these conditions for a diode-source network will be evident when the algorithm is described, as it will be shown to yield a solution whenever the two existence conditions are satisfied. Of course, the sufficiency also follows from the existence theorem of quadratic programming.

Suppose it is required that a certain network N of voltage and current sources, diodes, and resistors be solved. From this network a new network V may be obtained by removing all current sources and resistors. This network will be called the voltage reduced network associated with N. The voltage reduced network for the network in Fig. 4-12a is shown in Fig. 4-12b. Now every loop in the original network N which contained only voltage sources and diodes appears unaltered in the reduced network V. In fact, V contains only those loops. Hence a network N satisfies the first existence condition if and only if the associated reduced network V satisfies that condition. Note that the reduced network V always satisfies the second condition because it contains no current sources.

Similarly, we may form the current reduced network C from N by replacing all voltage sources and resistors in N by short circuits. The current reduced network for the network in Fig. 4-12a is shown in Fig. 4-12c. Then for any division of the nodes of N in which only diodes and current sources connect the two groups of nodes, the corresponding division of the nodes of C will yield the same situation. In fact, every division of the nodes of C corresponds to some such division of the nodes of N. Thus a network N satisfies the second existence condition if and only if the associated reduced network C satisfies that condition. Again, the reduced network C always satisfies the first condition because it contains no voltage sources.

Thus we have reached on the basis of electrical reasoning the conclusion stated in Chapter 3:

> A network made up of voltage and current sources, diodes and resistors possesses a solution if and only if the associated voltage reduced network and current reduced network both possess solutions.

First Algorithm for Diode-Source Networks

In this section the algorithm for solving any diode-source network satisfying the nonredundancy and existence conditions will be presented. Before describing the algorithm in step-by-step detail the equivalent operations performed on a real network will be discussed. This should give a good physical picture of how the algorithm proceeds. The method involves two distinct phases: In the first phase a solution of the voltage reduced network is found. In the second phase the result of the first phase is used as a starting point to form a complete solution of the network. In terms of linear programming, a feasible vector is found for the primal problem and is then modified until it is optimal. Physically, the algorithm amounts to assembling the components of the network in a rather particular manner as follows:

a)

b)

c)

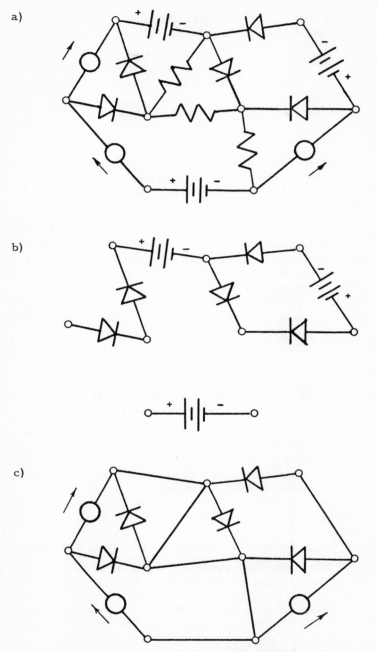

Fig. 4-12 Diode-source-resistor network and its
associated reduced networks

58

<u>Phase I</u>
1) Start with only the voltage sources.
2) Add the diodes one at a time.

<u>Phase II</u>
3) Short circuit sufficient diodes so that the short circuits and the voltage sources form a full tree of the complete network.
4) Add the current sources one at a time.
5) Restore the diodes which were short-circuited in Step 3 one at a time.

In the following description, the network consisting of those components which have already been "assembled" according to the above procedure will be called the <u>solved subnetwork</u>. Thus at each step in the algorithm one has a set of branch currents and voltages which form a solution of the pertinent solved subnetwork. By following the order of assembly given above it is always possible, as will be demonstrated below, to find a solution for the combination of the solved subnetwork and the next component to be added. This statement is true only if the network to be solved satisfies the nonredundancy and existence conditions given above.

In the figures the letters C, B, and O will be used to indicate that a diode is in the closed, breakpoint, or open state, respectively.

<u>Phase I: Solving the voltage reduced network</u>
<u>Step 1)</u> Select as the initial solved network a full tree of the network being solved by
    (a) including all voltage source branches
    (b) adding sufficient diode branches so that every node is covered while producing no loops.

It is readily apparent that such a tree exists. According to the first nonredundancy assumption, there is no possible division of the nodes of the network into two groups such that only current sources connect members of the two groups. This assures that there is a tree of the network containing only voltage sources and diodes. The second nonredundancy assumption states that there are no loops containing only voltage sources. This assures the existence of a full tree containing diodes and all voltage sources. A diode-source network and a full tree for it with a potential distribution are shown in Fig. 4-13.

<u>Step 2)</u> Consider each diode of the initial solved network as being in the breakpoint state (zero voltage, zero current). Compute a consistent set of node potentials for this network (tree). Consider all diodes whose voltage is zero or greater than zero as part of the solved subnetwork and in the breakpoint or open state, respectively.

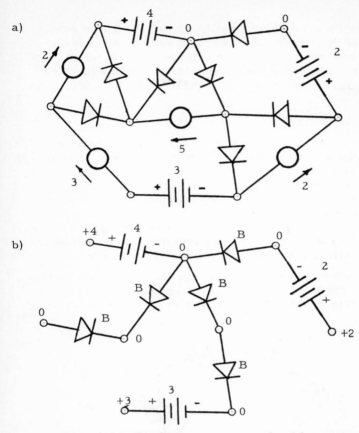

Fig. 4-13 Diode-source network with tree and potential
distribution for starting Phase I

This may be done by setting the potential of an arbitrarily chosen
initial node equal to zero. Then compute the potentials of those
nodes connected to the initial node by a branch of the tree. This
will allow the potentials of other nodes to be evaluated from values
previously computed. Continuance of the process will lead to the
assignment of a potential value to each node of the network. Since
by definition a tree contains no loops, no inconsistency can ever
arise: that is, it is always possible to compute the required set
of node potentials.

Step 3) Select a diode not in the solved subnetwork. If
there is none, Phase I is complete and the present
set of node potentials forms a solution of the voltage
reduced network. Proceed with Phase II. If there
is such a diode, designate the nodes on which its
plus and minus terminals are incident by P and M,
respectively. Let E be the magnitude of the (negative) voltage of the selected diode.

In Steps 4, 5, 6, and 7 a solution will be found for a new subnetwork consisting of the solved subnetwork plus the diode chosen in Step 3. The method involves "labelling" those nodes at which current is "available" over some path from node P. At the termination of the labelling, a new solution is indicated which is nearer to satisfying the diode selected in Step 3.

<u>Step 4)</u> Label node P.

<u>Step 5)</u> Label node j if node i is labelled and there is a branch of the subnetwork connecting nodes i and j which is
    i) a voltage source
    ii) a diode in the breakpoint state directed from node i to node j
Repeat until no more nodes can be labelled. If node M is not labelled proceed with Step 6. If node M is labelled, the network possesses no solution.

In the latter case there is a path between the plus and minus terminals of the chosen diode containing only voltage sources and breakpoint diodes (See Fig. 4-14). Together with the selected diode the

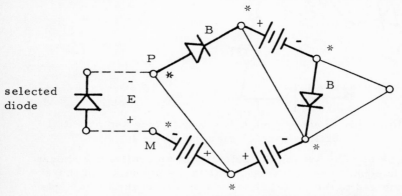

Fig. 4-14 The situation if node M is labelled

branches of this path form a loop containing only voltage sources and similarly aligned diodes with the total loop voltage equal to E. The first existence condition is thereby violated and the network has no solution.

If node M is not labelled, then the nodes of the network can be divided into two groups, labelled and unlabelled. Any branch running from a labelled node i to an unlabelled node j must be

    i) a diode in the open state
    ii) a breakpoint diode directed from node j to node i

The situation is illustrated in Fig. 4-15. If this were not true, the labelling operation, Step 5, was not completed. Remember that in

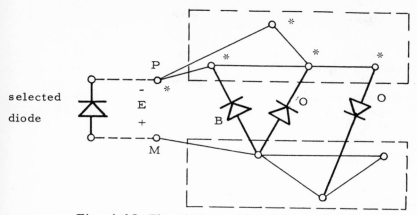

Fig. 4-15 The situation if node M is not labelled

Phase I there are no diodes in the closed state because all currents remain zero.

Now visualize simultaneously raising the values of the potentials on all of the labelled nodes by the amount ΔU. The new set of potentials will constitute a solution for the solved subnetwork as long as it is consistent with the demands of the individual branches. Those branches which join a pair of labelled nodes or join a pair of unlabelled nodes will be unaffected by the change. There are two classes of branches which connect labelled nodes with unlabelled nodes: breakpoint diodes and open diodes. In the case of the breakpoint diodes, they will change to the open state for any value of ΔU greater than zero, and will be satisfied no matter how large ΔU is. Open diodes directed from unlabelled nodes to labelled nodes will remain satisfied for any positive value of ΔU. For each open diode directed toward an unlabelled node, however, there is a limit on the allowable increase in the potential of the labelled node. The amount of this limit is equal to the voltage for the particular diode. Since, by our convention, the voltage for an open diode is never zero, there will always be some amount ΔU by which the potentials of the labelled nodes may be raised which will yield a new solution of the solved subnetwork. This increase of potentials will make the voltage of the chosen diode more positive and bring it nearer to being satisfied. The precise operations are as follows.

Step 6) Consider those diodes in the subnetwork which are in the open state and directed from a labelled node to an unlabelled node. Let ΔV be the smallest voltage for any of these diodes. If ΔV is greater than E or there are no open diodes directed toward unlabelled nodes, set ΔU = E, otherwise set ΔU = ΔV.

Step 7) Increase the potentials of the labelled nodes by ΔU. Every breakpoint diode connecting a labelled node with an unlabelled node switches to the open state. Some open diodes directed toward unlabelled nodes from labelled ones may enter the breakpoint state. All other diodes of the subnetwork retain their former state. After the potential change some diodes not in the solved subnetwork may no longer have negative voltages. Consider these diodes as part of the solved subnetwork in future steps. If $\Delta U = E$ a solution has been obtained for a new subnetwork consisting of the old subnetwork plus the selected diode. Remove all labels and go back to Step 3. Otherwise set $E = E - \Delta U$ and return to Step 5.

Each time a potential change is executed in Steps 6 and 7, either a solution is found satisfying the selected diode, or one of the open diodes joining a labelled node to an unlabelled node moves to the breakpoint state. If the latter is the case another node can always be labelled in Step 5. Therefore, for each diode chosen in Step 3, the number of labelling operations before the diode can be satisfied can never exceed the number of nodes in the network. Thus Phase I must terminate in a finite number of steps.

Phase II: The completion of the solution

Step 1) Consider any division of the nodes of the voltage reduced network into two groups such that the only branches joining members of the two groups are diodes in the open state. Raise or lower the potentials of one of the groups of nodes until at least one of the open diodes changes to the breakpoint state. Repeat until no division of the nodes as above is possibl

The object of Step 1 is to insure that it is possible to find a tree with the properties requested in Step 2. It is clear that each change of potentials in Step 1 gives a new set of potential values which is a solution of the voltage reduced network. For each change of potentials at least one diode changes from the open to the breakpoint state, while all breakpoint diodes remain at breakpoint. Hence Step 1 must terminate in a number of repetitions not greater than the initial number of open diodes.

Step 2) Select from the voltage reduced network a full tree consisting only of voltage sources and breakpoint diodes. Assign a current distribution to the branches of this tree which satisfies the continuity condition and meets the requirements of the current sources. Identify those diodes of the tree which have currents greater than zero as being in the closed state. Short circuit those diodes in the tree which have current less than zero. The resulting network (with the current sources) is the solved subnetwork used as the starting point for the iterations of Phase II.

The process of assigning the current distribution to the tree might be carried out as follows. Select a current source and a path from the tree connecting the pair of nodes on which the current source is incident. Add the current demanded by the current source to the current in each branch aligned with the path. Subtract this current from the other branches in the path. Repeat for each current source. This method also shows that such an assignment is always possible. Fig. 4-16a shows a solution of the voltage reduced network obtained from the network of Fig. 4-13. Fig. 4-16b shows a tree satisfying the requirements of Step 2 with a current distribution satisfying the current source requirements

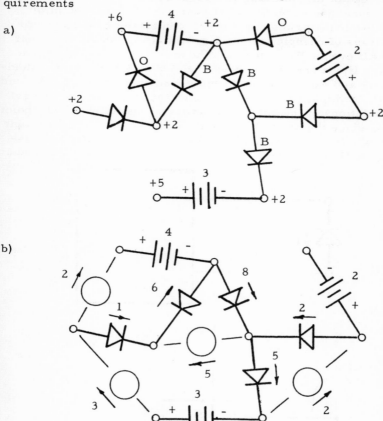

a)

b)

Fig. 4-16 Solution of voltage reduced network and current distribution for starting Phase II

Step 3) Select one of the diodes which is short circuited. If no short circuits remain, the present set of branch currents and voltages constitutes a solution of the network and Phase II of the algorithm has been completed. Otherwise, designate the nodes on which the plus and minus terminals of the selected diode are incident by P and M respectively. Denote the magnitude of the (reverse) current through this diode by I.

In Steps 4 through 9 a solution will be produced for a new network consisting of the solved subnetwork with the short circuit removed from the diode selected in Step 3. Again nodes are labelled for which current is available over paths from node P. As a consequence of the labelling, one of the following two results occur: Either a path is produced connecting nodes P and M over which an increment of current can flow bringing the current between these nodes closer to zero, or a means of changing the node potentials is indicated so that such a path will eventually be found. The meaning of this statement will be clearer if one considers nodes P and M as terminals of a diode-source network and examines the possible combinations of current and voltage at this terminal pair. As was indicated in Chapter 3, the set of terminal solutions of the solved subnetwork constitutes a breakpoint curve. Also, since the network contains no resistors, the breakpoint curve contains only horizontal and vertical line segments as is illustrated in Fig. 4-17. Initially terminals P and M are short circuited and

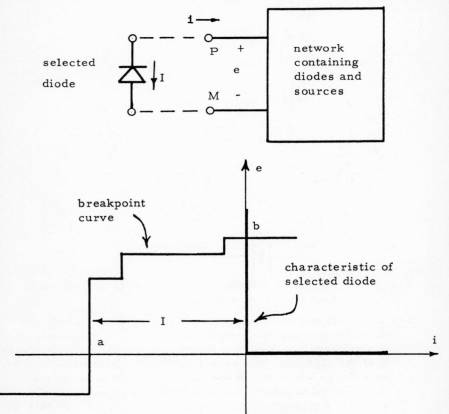

Fig. 4-17 Breakpoint curve of the solved subnetwork
viewed from the selected diode

the network stands at point a in the figure. Point b is the intersection of the curves describing the relations imposed by the diode
and by the network. Steps 4 through 9 move the solution of the solved
network from point a to point b by "tracing" the breakpoint curve.
The potential changes correspond to vertical motions on the curve:
each increment of current along a path corresponds to a horizontal
movement.

Step 4) Label node P. Label node j if node i is labelled
and there is a branch connecting i and j which is
   i) a voltage source
   ii) a diode in the closed state
   iii) a breakpoint diode directed toward node j
   iv) a short circuit

Repeat until no more nodes can be labelled. If node M is
labelled, proceed with Step 5. If not, go to Step 8.

If node M is labelled the situation is as shown in Fig. 4-18.

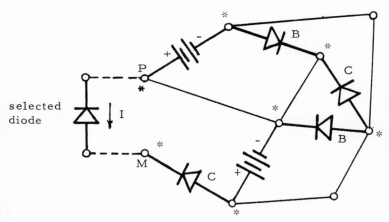

Fig. 4-18 The situation if node M is labelled

Step 5) Select a path running from node P to node M which contains only voltage sources, closed diodes, and breakpoint
diodes aligned with the direction of the path.

Such a path must exist or else node M could never have been labelled.
Now consider increasing the current through the branches of the path
by the amount ΔJ. If the potentials are held constant, only the branches
of the path will be affected by this change. Thus the new current distribution, together with the branch voltages, will still be a solution as
long as the branches of the path remain satisfied. The voltage sources
in the path will allow an arbitrary amount of current to flow, hence
they impose no restriction on ΔJ. The breakpoint diodes and the closed

diodes aligned with the direction of the path also allow an arbitrary increase in current. On the other hand, each closed diode oriented against the path places a limit on the amount of increase in current along the path. Each of these diodes will allow an amount of increase equal to the present current through the diode. The algorithm proceeds as follows:

Step 6) Consider those diodes of the path selected in Step 5 which are in the closed state and are oriented against the direction of the path. Let ΔH be the smallest current for any of these diodes. If ΔH is greater than I, or there are no closed diodes oriented against the direction of the path, set $\Delta J = I$. Otherwise set $\Delta J = \Delta H$.

Step 7) For each branch of the path, increase the current by ΔJ if it is aligned with the path, or decrease the current by ΔJ if it is not aligned. Each breakpoint diode in the path shifts to the closed state. Some of the closed diodes may move to the breakpoint state. Some short-circuited diodes may no longer have negative currents. Remove the short circuit for any such diode. If $\Delta J = I$ a solution of the subnetwork has been found which satisfies the selected diode. Consider a new subnetwork in which this diode is no longer short circuited. Remove all labels and return to Step 3. Otherwise set $I = I - \Delta J$, remove all labels and return to Step 4.

If node M is not labelled, the situation is as indicated in Fig. 4-19. Again consider raising the potentials of the labelled nodes by the amount

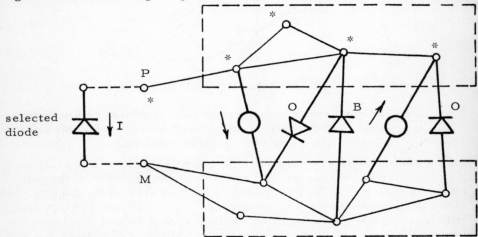

Fig. 4-19 The situation if node M is not labelled

ΔV as in Steps 6 and 7 of Phase I. This time each branch joining a labelled node i to an unlabelled node j must be

i) a diode in the open state
ii) a breakpoint diode directed from node j to node i
iii) a current source

Otherwise node j should have been labelled. As before the open diodes directed toward unlabelled nodes determine the amount by which the potentials may be raised and still constitute, with the branch currents, a solution of the solved subnetwork.

Step 8) Consider those open diodes of the solved subnetwork which are directed towards unlabelled nodes. If there are none, the problem possesses no solution. Let ΔV be the smallest voltage for any of these open diodes.

If there are no open diodes directed toward unlabelled nodes, then all diodes joining labelled nodes with unlabelled nodes are directed toward the labelled nodes. Also the sum of values of the current sources connecting labelled with unlabelled nodes must be exactly I, that is, greater than zero and directed in the conduction direction of the diodes. The second existence condition is therefore violated and no solution of the network exists.

Step 9) Increase the potential of each labelled node by ΔV. Each breakpoint diode connecting a labelled node to an unlabelled node will switch to the open state. At least one open diode will move to its breakpoint. Remove all labels and return to Step 4.

For each change in either the potential distribution or the branch current distribution during Steps 4 through 9 of Phase II, at least one diode of the solved subnetwork changes state. Also each change in potentials or currents moves the solution point uniformly upward or to the right along the breakpoint curve. Therefore no given combination of diode states can ever be repeated. This assures that the iterations terminate in a finite number of steps, with either a solution or a demonstration that no solutions exist.

Second Algorithm for Diode-Source Networks

The algorithm described in the previous section first produced a solution of the voltage reduced network corresponding to a given diode-source network. In this section a second algorithm will be described which first obtains a solution of the associated current reduced network. In mathematical programming terminology, a feasible vector is found for the dual linear program and is modified until it becomes optimal.

The second algorithm is equivalent to performing the following operations on the physical diode-source network.

Phase I: Solving the current reduced network

1) Replace all diodes and voltage sources of the network by short circuits. Thus the starting network contains only current sources.

2) Exchange each diode with the corresponding short circuit, one at a time until all diodes have been repositioned
in the network.

Phase II: Completing the solution
3) Remove all diodes from the network which have zero
current through them.

4) Exchange the voltage sources for their corresponding
short circuits one at a time.

5) Restore the diodes that were removed in 3), one at a time.

The precise procedure is given below. The description has been
shortened as the principles are essentially the same as in the first
algorithm.

Phase I: Solving the current reduced network
Steps 1 and 2) Select a tree from the current reduced network
which contains none of the current sources. Assign a current distribution to this tree which satisfies the current
source requirements. Short circuit those diodes of the tree
which have reverse (negative) current. The resulting network is the initial solved subnetwork for Phase I.

Step 3) Select one of the short-circuited diodes. If none, Phase
I is complete and the present current distribution is a solution of the current reduced network. Proceed with Phase II.
If there is a short-circuited diode, let P and M represent
the plus and minus nodes for this diode. Let I be the reverse current through this diode.

Step 4) Label node P.

Step 5) Label node j if node i is labelled and there is a branch
joining nodes i and j which is
    i) a diode in the closed state
    ii) a breakpoint diode directed toward node j
    iii) a short circuit

Repeat until no more nodes can be labelled. If node M is
labelled, proceed with Step 6. If not, the network possesses
no solution.

If M is not labelled, the second existence condition is violated.

Step 6) Select a path from node P to node M made up of closed
diodes and breakpoint diodes aligned with the path. Let ΔH
be the smallest current of the closed diodes aligned against
the path. If $\Delta H \geq \Delta I$ or there are no such closed diodes,
set $\Delta J = \Delta I$. Otherwise set $\Delta J = \Delta H$.

Step 7) For each branch of the path, increase the branch current by ΔJ if it is aligned with the path, decrease by ΔJ if
it is not. Each breakpoint diode in the path will become
closed. Some of the closed diodes aligned against the path
may move to the breakpoint state. After the change in the
current distribution some of the short circuited diodes may
no longer have negative currents. Remove the short circuits
from these diodes and consider them part of the solved subnetwork. Remove all labels. If ΔJ = I, go back to Step 3,
otherwise return to Step 4.

Phase II: Completing the solution
Step 1) Consider any loop of the current reduced network which,
with the current distribution given by Phase I, contains only
diodes in the closed state. If there are none, proceed with
Step 2. Modify the currents in the branches of the loop by
adding an increment ΔI to each branch aligned with the loop
and subtracting ΔI from each branch aligned against the loop,
so that one of the diodes moves to the breakpoint state. Repeat Step 1 until all such loops are eliminated.

This assures that a tree as required in Step 2 does exist.

Step 2) Select a full tree for the current reduced network by
(a) including all closed diodes and short circuits
(b) adding sufficient breakpoint diodes to form a full tree
Reinsert the voltage sources which were replaced by short
circuits in forming the current reduced network. Compute
a set of node potentials which satisfies the voltage sources
and the other branches of the tree. This tree plus the current
sources forms the initial solved subnetwork for Phase II. Add
to and consider as part of the solved subnetwork any diodes
not in the tree which do not have negative voltage.

Step 3) Select a diode not in the solved subnetwork. If there are
none the present branch currents and voltages form a solution
of the entire network and Phase II has been completed. If
there is such a diode, let P and M designate the node on which
its plus and minus terminals are incident. Denote by E the
magnitude of the (negative) voltage of this diode.

In Steps 4 through 9 of the second algorithm a solution is produced for
a new subnetwork consisting of the solved subnetwork plus the diode selected in Step 3. The method, as in the first algorithm, is by tracing
the breakpoint curve observed between nodes P and M. The steps are
identical to those in Phase II of the first algorithm except for the following alterations.

(a) In figuring the change in current in a path from node P to node
M in Step 6, ΔJ is always set equal to ΔH. If there are no closed diodes
directed against the path, the network has no solutions by violation of
the first existence condition.

(b) In figuring the amount of potential change in Step 8, set ΔV
equal to E if ΔV is greater than E or there are no open diodes directed
from labelled nodes to unlabelled nodes.

(c) In Step 9 the change in potentials may remove the negative
voltages from some diodes not in the solved subnetwork. Include
these diodes in the solved subnetwork for future steps. Remove all
labels. If ΔV = E include the selected diode in the solved subnetwork
and return to Step 3. Otherwise go to Step 4.

(d) In Step 7 change the currents by ΔJ, set I = I - ΔJ, remove
all labels and return to Step 4.

Similar arguments to those given in the previous section demonstrate
that this procedure also will terminate in a finite number of steps.

Altering Solution for New Parameter Values

One appropriate question concerning these algorithms is this: Given
a solution for some diode-source network, how easy is it to find a solution for the same network but with different values of the current and
voltage sources? Does one have to start over from the beginning of
the algorithm or can one make use of the previous solution?

In the case of the algorithms described above, the previous solution
is readily used as a starting point for forming a new solution. Three
cases are evident depending on whether the current sources, the voltage
sources, or both take on new values.

Case I) Suppose that only current source values differ between the
new and previous networks. Select a full tree of the network which, for
the current and voltage values for the old solution, contains all voltage
sources and all closed diodes, plus sufficient breakpoint diodes to form
a complete tree. Assign a current distribution to the tree such that the
new current source requirements are met. Keep the old set of node
potentials. Some diodes of the tree may now have negative currents.
Use the procedure of Phase II of the first algorithm to satisfy these
diodes and thus obtain the new solution of the network.

Case II) Suppose that only voltage source values differ between the
new and previous networks. Select a full tree of the network which, for
the current and voltage values of the old solution, contains all voltage
sources and all closed diodes, plus sufficient breakpoint diodes to complete the tree. Keep the previous distribution of branch currents but
compute a set of node potentials that satisfies the branches of the tree
for the new voltage source values. Some diodes not in the tree may
not have negative voltage. Apply the method of Phase II of the second
algorithm to satisfy these diodes and produce the solution of the new
network.

That a full tree with the right properties to start these procedures
can always be found is assured by the nonredundancy assumptions. Suppose that the nodes of the network could be divided into two groups such
that any branches connecting nodes in both groups is either an open
diode or a current source. This situation could prohibit the existence

of the required tree. The first nonredundancy assumption assures
that not all of these branches are current sources. Therefore the
potentials of one of the groups of nodes could be altered so that one
of the open diodes moves to the breakpoint state. On the other hand,
suppose that the set of branches containing all of the voltage sources
and all closed diodes contained a loop. This also could prohibit the
construction of the required tree. However, the second nonredundancy assumption assures that such a loop does not contain voltage
sources only. Therefore the currents in the branches of the loop
can be altered so that a closed diode moves to the breakpoint state.
These considerations insure that given a diode-source network and
a solution, either a full tree containing all of the voltage sources and
all closed diodes, plus sufficient breakpoint diodes, can be selected,
or the solution can be easily modified so that such a tree can be
selected.

Case III) Suppose both voltage source and current source values
are different in the new network. Consider an intermediate network
in which only the current source values have been changed from those
in the previous network. Solve this network by the method indicated
under Case I. Now change the voltage source values and proceed as
under Case II. The intermediate network is always solvable if the
new network has a solution. This is true because the voltage reduced
network for the intermediate problem is identical to that of the previous problem while the current reduced network for the intermediate
problem is identical to the one for the new problem. The former must
possess a solution if the previous network was solvable, and the latter
must possess solutions if the new network is solvable. Hence the
intermediate network must also be solvable.

An alternate way of handling Case III problems is to solve an intermediate network in which only the voltage source values are changed
and subsequently to modify this solution for the new current source
values. As above the intermediate network will always be solvable.

Application of the Algorithms to Flow Problems

As an illustration of the application of these methods to flow problems,
let us return to the shortest path problem described at the beginning of
the chapter. As pointed out there, the shortest path may be found from
a solution of a diode-source network which is redrawn in Fig. 4-20. An

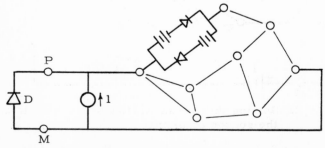

Fig. 4-20 Solving the shortest path problem with
the first algorithm

extra diode has been included which clearly cannot alter the solution of the network. Since the voltage sources have positive values, there is an obvious solution to the voltage reduced network: namely, with zero potential on all major nodes. An initial solution for starting Phase II of the first algorithm can be obtained by simply routing the unit current from the sole current source through the extra diode D in the reverse direction. This diode is then the only unsatisfied diode in the network. Hence, tracing the breakpoint curve observed at the indicated terminal pair will yield a complete solution when the terminal current reaches zero.

In applying the second algorithm to the shortest path problem, a solution for the current reduced network may be found by choosing an arbitrary path through the reduced network and assigning the unit current to this path as indicated in Fig. 4-21. Since it is trivial to choose

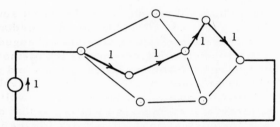

Fig. 4-21 Solving the shortest path problem with the second algorithm

the path so that current passes through each diode in the forward direction, no further steps are required. Upon inserting the voltage sources to initiate Phase II, reverse voltages may be impressed on certain diodes not in the chosen path. Steps 4 through 9 of Phase II must be employed to modify the solution so that these diodes become satisfied.

Similar remarks apply to the electrical model for the maximum flow problem shown in Fig. 4-22. Here a solution of the current reduced

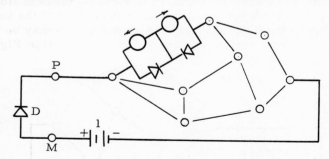

Fig. 4-22 Solving the maximum flow problem with the second algorithm

network is available by inspection: The currents are simply routed through the diodes connected in parallel with the sources. An initial solution for starting Phase II of the second algorithm would be with the unit voltage impressed across the extra diode D. Tracing the breakpoint curve observed at the terminals of this diode produces a solution of the network when the terminal voltage reaches zero, and hence the maximum possible flow. It is evident that this is precisely the dual (topologically) of the first method for the shortest distance problem.

A dual for the other shortest path algorithm can also be constructed. A solution of the voltage reduced network can be found by selecting an arbitrary cut set of the network (a set of branches which interrupts all paths through the network) and assigning 1-volt potentials to the nodes to the left of the cut set and zero potentials to those on the right. This is indicated in Fig. 4-23. To initiate Phase II of the first algorithm, route the source currents through the diodes connected in

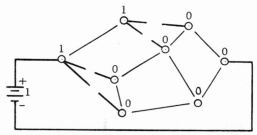

Fig. 4-23 Solving the maximum flow problem with the first algorithm

shunt with them except for one source in each branch of the cut set. The currents of these remaining sources must be assigned to a loop in the network that includes the unit voltage source. These currents may have to be assigned in the reverse direction through some diodes. Tracing the breakpoint curves for these diodes by following Phase II of the first algorithm will solve the network and indicate the maximum possible flow.

Now consider the general case of a capacitated network with a unit cost assigned to each branch. The electrical model for this case was shown in Fig. 4-7. For illustration it is convenient to alter the network model as shown in Fig. 4-24 so that all flow is routed through a common source node and a common sink node. If the main source has a value equal to the total flow required through the network, it is clear that the first model and the altered one are equivalent: A voltage and current distribution in the capacitated branches is a solution of one if and only if it is a solution of the other.

If all unit costs in the original network flow problem are positive, all batteries in Fig. 4-24 will have positive values. Then zero

74

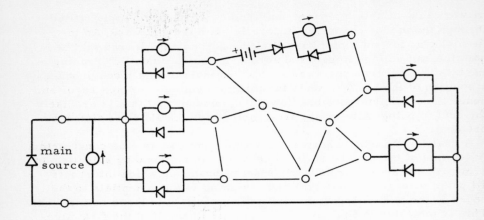

Fig. 4-24 Solving the general network flow problem
with the diode-source model

potentials on all major nodes is a trivial solution of the voltage reduced network associated with the model. An initial current distribution for starting Phase II of the first algorithm is readily obtained
by routing each source current through the diode connected in shunt
with it. The only unsatisfied diode is the one shunting the main
source. Tracing its breakpoint curve will produce the least-cost
solution for the flow problem. Applied to the flow problem in this
particular manner, this is exactly the Ford-Fulkerson method for
the transportation problem [15] generalized to the capacitated network flow problem.

Of course, the algorithms described here are more flexible than
are indicated by the above applications to very special networks.
Actually a sufficiently wide choice of initial solutions is allowed, so
that a previous solution of the same network for different data (current source and voltage source values) may readily be used as an
initial solution. The method is also more general, for it is capable
of solving any diode-source network, which would appear to be a
larger class of problems than the class of capacitated network flow
problems. In particular, the method will handle flow problems in
which negative unit costs may be specified or lower bounds placed
on the allowable flow in any branch. The Ford-Fulkerson method is
not designed to handle these features.

Network Flow Problems with Quadratic Costs

The electrical model for network flow problems can be extended
to include flow branches for which the total cost contains terms dependent on the square of the individual branch flows. Such a branch is
indicated in Fig. 4-25 along with its electrical model. The quadratic
cost coefficient appears as a resistance in the model. The correctness of the model may be verified by comparison with the primal

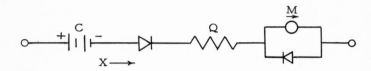

$$= CX + \frac{1}{2} QX^2 \qquad 0 \le X \le M$$

Fig. 4-25 Quadratic cost flow branch and its
electrical analogue

formulation for diode-source-resistor networks given in Chapter
3 (pp. 31-34). Thus network flow problems with quadratic components of cost could be solved by an algorithm for solving diode-
source-resistor networks. It appears that the algorithms presented in this chapter could be generalized to permit resistance
branches by employing topological methods [27] to evaluate incremental solutions of the network. These methods, however, are
combinatorial in character and could require prohibitive calculation time, even on relatively simple networks. Certainly the simplicity and elegance of the diode-source algorithms would be ab-
sent. It would seem that the most practical means of attacking
flow problems with quadratic costs would be to approximate the
cost curve with a piece-wise linear curve and substitute an appropriate number of linear cost branches connected in parallel. Minty
[25] has considered a similar method for solving networks of nonlinear resistors by first approximating each resistor voltage-
current characteristic by a breakpoint curve made up of only
horizontal and vertical line segments. This is equivalent to replacing each resistor by a particular diode-source network.

Chapter 5

A BREAKPOINT TRACING PROCEDURE

At the end of Chapter 3 the terminal-pair system of equations

	η	x	ξ	y	v	
		A	e			b
	-Q		A^T	I		c
	1		e^T			0

(5-1a)

in which the variables x and v are required to satisfy the complementary slackness condition

$$x \geq 0, \quad v \geq 0, \quad v^T x = 0 \tag{5-1b}$$

was introduced. It was pointed out (and proved in Appendix G) that the solutions of such a system form a breakpoint curve in the ξ-η plane. In this chapter an algebraic method will be developed for "tracing" the breakpoint curve corresponding to a terminal-pair system. In Chapter 6 this method will be applied to general linear and quadratic programs.

A second form of terminal-pair system

	ξ	y	η	x	v	
	A^T	e			I	c
	-Q		A			b
	1		e^T			0

(5-2)

and several other variations of 5-1 will also be employed in connection with the methods presented in Chapter 6. The sets of terminal solutions for all these variations have the same properties as are demonstrated in Appendix G for 5-1. The breakpoint tracing algorithm is formulated here with reference to the system 5-1, but the method applies with little modification to any of the variations.

The details of the recursion formulae to be developed for the breakpoint-stepping algorithm are quite similar to those of the well-known simplex method for linear programming [9]. As we shall see, here, as in the simplex method, the central idea is the single elimination step of the Gauss-Jordan reduction for systems of linear equations.

The Electrical Model of the Terminal-Pair System

Again, the electrical analogy will be employed to give a physical interpretation of the method. The terminal-pair system 5-1 has the electrical model shown in Fig. 5-1. The primal variables ξ and x are represented by currents in the model while the dual variables η, y, and v are represented by voltages. The m-by-n rectangular matrix A becomes a rectangular array of ideal d-c transformers, and Q becomes an array of resistors. The column matrix e appears as a column of transformers with their secondaries connected in series. Voltage and current sources form the analog of the right-hand side of the terminal-pair system. In Fig. 5-2 the diagram has been repeated, simplified by the use of symbols to represent arrays of transformers, resistors, diodes, and sources. Heavy lines in the figure mean that many electrical circuits are represented, while a light line means a single circuit is represented. These same conventions will be used in Chapter 6 where electrical models are constructed for general linear and quadratic programs.

The "black box" representation of the electrical model shown in Fig. 5-3 will be employed in developing the breakpoint tracing scheme. Here all circuit elements with the exception of the n diodes are represented by a "black box" with $n + 1$ terminal pairs. One of the terminal pairs is the terminal pair of the original network with current ξ and voltage η. The diodes appear at the remaining n terminal pairs and have currents $x_1, \ldots, x_n$ and voltages $v_1, \ldots, v_n$. The variables y must now be regarded as unobservable voltages inside the black box.

Basic Solutions

For convenience the letter P will be used in this chapter to designate the matrix of a terminal-pair system

$$P = [P_\eta \ P_X \ P_\xi \ P_Y \ P_V] = \begin{bmatrix} 0 & A & e & 0 & 0 \\ 0 & -Q & 0 & A^T & I \\ 1 & 0 & 0 & e^T & 0 \end{bmatrix}$$

and the column vectors of variables and constants of the system will be denoted by

$$z = \begin{bmatrix} \eta \\ x \\ \xi \\ y \\ v \end{bmatrix} \qquad \text{and} \qquad d = \begin{bmatrix} b \\ c \\ 0 \end{bmatrix}$$

79

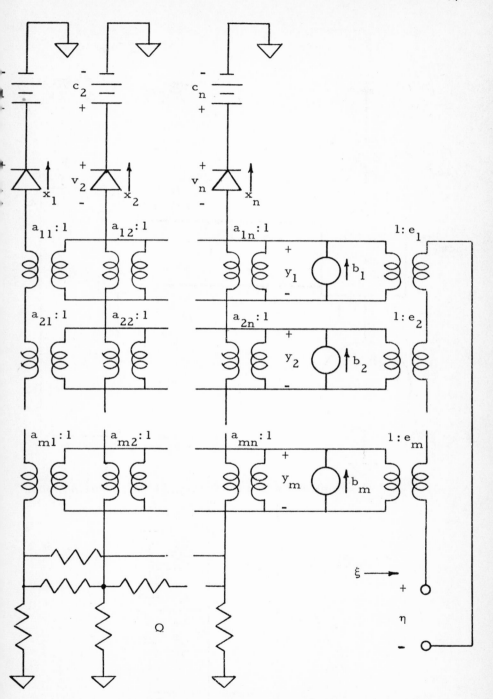

Fig. 5-1 Electrical model of the terminal-pair system

80

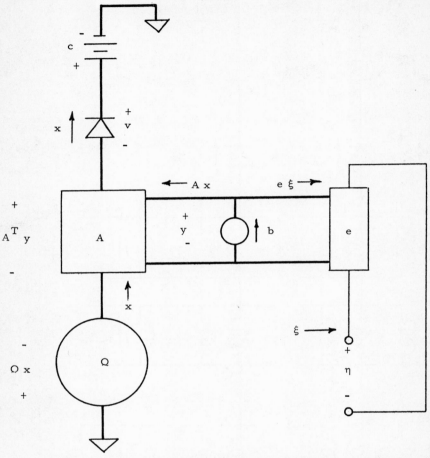

Fig. 5-2 Simplified drawing of terminal-pair system model

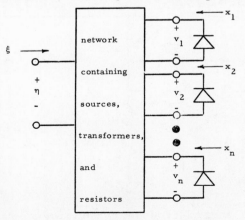

Fig. 5-3 Black box representation of the terminal-pair system

With this notation, the equations of the terminal-pair system become

$$P z = d \qquad (5-3)$$

The pair of variables (x_i, v_i) associated with the ith diode of the electrical model will be called a <u>conjugate variable pair</u>. Certain solutions of a terminal-pair system called <u>basic solutions</u> are particularly important in the tracing procedure. These solutions correspond to the changes in slope or <u>breakpoints</u> of the breakpoint curve. Specifically:

A <u>basis</u> of a terminal-pair system is a set B of $m + n + 1$ linearly independent columns of P which includes P_η, P_ξ, and all the P_{y_i}, but does not contain both P_{x_i} and P_{v_i} for any i

A <u>basic solution</u> of a terminal-pair system is a solution $\bar{z}$ in which the only non-zero components of $\bar{x}$ and $\bar{v}$ correspond to vectors in some basis of the system.

Since the vectors P_η, P_ξ, and P_{y_i} are in every basis, exactly $n - 1$ of the vectors P_{x_i} and P_{v_i} must be members of each basis. In terms of the electrical model, this means that in any basic solution at least one of the diodes must have both $x_i = 0$ and $v_i = 0$, that is, must be in the breakpoint state, and we will say that this conjugate variable pair is <u>at breakpoint</u>. For the present it will be assumed that any basic solution has only one diode (conjugate variable pair) at breakpoint. The contrary is a possible situation, but it is a <u>degenerate</u> condition and will be considered later.

The column vectors of a basis form an $m + n + 1^{th}$ order square matrix. Since it was stipulated that the basis vectors were linearly independent, this matrix possesses an inverse. Let the <u>row</u> of this inverse matrix S^T corresponding to the column P_i of the <u>basis</u> be represented by the <u>column</u> vector S_i. Then

$$P_i^T S_j = \begin{cases} 1 & i = j \\ 0 & i \neq j \end{cases} \qquad i, j \text{ in B} \qquad (5-4)$$

because the product of a matrix with its inverse is the identity matrix.

By means of the vectors of the basis inverse, any column of P not in the basis may be expressed as a linear combination of basis vectors, namely

$$P_j = I P_j = [\sum_{i \text{ in B}} P_i S_i^T] P_j$$

$$(5-5)$$

$$= \sum_{i \text{ in B}} (S_i^T P_j) P_i$$

Unit Solutions: Superposition

Let b indicate the diode which is at breakpoint for a basic solution $\bar{z}$ with basis $\bar{B}$ and inverse $\bar{S}^T$. Consider the two variable vectors

$$
\overset{o}{z} =
\begin{bmatrix}
\overset{o}{\eta} \\
\overset{o}{x} \\
\overset{o}{\xi} \\
\overset{o}{y} \\
\overset{o}{v}
\end{bmatrix}
\qquad \text{and} \qquad
\overset{*}{z} =
\begin{bmatrix}
\overset{*}{\eta} \\
\overset{*}{x} \\
\overset{*}{\xi} \\
\overset{*}{y} \\
\overset{*}{v}
\end{bmatrix}
$$

associated with the <u>nonbasic</u> variables x_b and v_b respectively. These vectors are defined by

$$
\overset{o}{z}_i =
\begin{cases}
-\bar{S}_i^T P_r & \text{i in } \bar{B} \\
1 & \text{i} = r \\
0 & \text{other i}
\end{cases}
\tag{5-6}
$$

and

$$
\overset{*}{z}_i =
\begin{cases}
-\bar{S}_i^T P_h & \text{i in } \bar{B} \\
1 & \text{i} = h \\
0 & \text{other i}
\end{cases}
\tag{5-7}
$$

where P_r and P_h are the columns of P associated with x_b and v_b, respectively. It follows that

$$
P \overset{o}{z} = \sum_i \overset{o}{z}_i P_i
$$

$$
= P_r - \sum_{i \text{ in } \bar{B}} (\bar{S}_i^T P_r) P_i
\tag{5-8}
$$

$$
= 0
$$

by relation 5-5, and similarly

$$
P \overset{*}{z} = 0
$$

Thus $\overset{o}{z}$ and $\overset{*}{z}$ are solutions of the terminal-pair system equations with the constant terms on the right set to zero. In terms of the electrical model $\overset{o}{z}$ and $\overset{*}{z}$ are <u>incremental</u> <u>solutions</u> of the network in the black box. That is, they are solutions of the black box when the current and voltage sources are "dead." Moreover, if the diodes which are in the open state for the basic solution $\bar{z}$ are replaced by open circuits and the closed diodes replaced by a short circuit, then $\overset{o}{z}$ is an incremental solution of this network in which a current of one ampere is forced in the terminal pair of the breakpoint diode while the voltage across this diode is maintained equal to zero by proper choice of $\overset{o}{\xi}$ and $\overset{o}{\eta}$. This is illustrated in Fig. 5-4a. Similarly, $\overset{*}{z}$ is an incremental solution in which a unit voltage is applied to the breakpoint terminal pair while $\overset{*}{\xi}$ and $\overset{*}{\eta}$ are selected so that

a)   b)

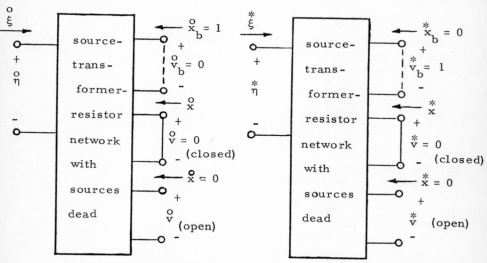

Fig. 5-4 Unit incremental solutions of a terminal-pair system

the current x_b is zero, as indicated in Fig. 5-4b. The incremental solutions $\overset{o}{z}$ and $\overset{*}{z}$ are therefore called the <u>unit solutions</u> associated with the basic solution $\bar{z}$ and the variables $\underline{x_b}$ and $\underline{v_b}$.

Now consider the variable vector formed by superimposing a positive multiple α of the unit solution $\overset{o}{z}$ on the basic solution $\bar{z}$:

$$z(\alpha) \;=\; \bar{z} + \alpha \overset{o}{z} \qquad\qquad (5\text{-}9)$$

Then, by using 5-3 and 5-8

$$P\,z(\alpha) \;=\; P\,\bar{z} + \alpha P \overset{o}{z} \;=\; d$$

Hence z is a solution of the terminal-pair system equations. But also

$$z_i(\alpha) = \begin{cases} \bar{z}_i - \alpha \bar{S}_i^T P_r & i \text{ in } \bar{B} \\ \alpha & i = r \\ 0 & \text{other } i \end{cases} \qquad (5\text{-}10)$$

Since $\bar{z}$ is a basic solution, it satisfies the complementary slackness conditions 5-1b. The only non-zero variable in $z(\alpha)$ which was zero in $\bar{z}$ is $z_r(\alpha) = x_b = \alpha$. But this also satisfies the complementary slackness condition because the variables pair (x_b, v_b) was at breakpoint in $\bar{z}$, P_{v_b} is not in the basis, and therefore $v_b(\alpha) = 0$.

Under the assumption that only one diode is ever at its breakpoint, each basic x_i or v_i must be greater than zero. As a consequence each x_i or v_i of the sum $z(\alpha)$ is greater than or equal to zero for some value of α greater than zero as long as it is not too large. Thus

$$z(\alpha) = \bar{z} + \alpha \overset{o}{z} \qquad (5\text{-}11)$$

is a solution of the terminal-pair system as long as α is less than some limiting value α which is greater than zero. This limiting value is given by

$$\overset{o}{\alpha} = \underset{i}{\text{Min}} \left[\frac{\bar{z}_i}{\bar{s}_i^T P_r} \right] \qquad \begin{array}{l} i \text{ corresponding to} \\ \text{columns of } P_X \text{ or} \\ P_V \text{ in } \bar{B} \text{ with} \end{array} \qquad (5\text{-}12)$$

$$\bar{s}_i^T P_r > 0$$

If there is no index i satisfying the condition given above, it follows that 5-10 gives a solution of the terminal-pair system for all positive values of α. This would mean that the last breakpoint of the system had been passed. Otherwise, for the value of α given by 5-12 one of the basic variables x_i or v_i will become zero. Denote the column of P associated with this variable by P_s. Then for the solution $z(\overset{o}{\alpha})$ diode b has moved away from its breakpoint, while some other diode has reached its breakpoint state. Hence $z(\overset{o}{\alpha})$ is a new basic solution in which the vector P_r has been added to the old basis and P_s dropped. The values of the basic variables in the new basic solution are given by the formulae

$$z_i = \begin{cases} \bar{z}_i - \dfrac{\bar{s}_i^T P_r}{\bar{s}_s^T P_r} \bar{z}_s , & i \neq r \\[4mm] & \qquad\qquad i \text{ in } B \qquad (5\text{-}13) \\[2mm] \dfrac{1}{\bar{s}_s^T P_r} \bar{z}_s , & i = r \end{cases}$$

where B contains the vectors of the new basis.

In the same way

$$z(\alpha) = \bar{z} + \alpha \overset{*}{z} \qquad (5\text{-}14)$$

is found to be a solution of the terminal-pair system for $0 \leq \alpha \leq \overset{*}{\alpha}$, where $\overset{*}{\alpha}$ is given by 5-12 with P_r replaced by P_h. Again $\bar{z}(\overset{*}{\alpha})$ is a new basic solution.

On the breakpoint curve of the terminal-pair system the two classes
of solutions formed by 5-6 and 5-7 correspond to motion along the
breakpoint curve in opposite directions away from the breakpoint associated with the basic solution $\bar{z}$. It is shown in Lemma G-7 that the
unit incremental solutions $\overset{o}{z}$ and $\overset{*}{z}$ must satisfy the relation

$$\overset{o}{\xi}\,\overset{*}{\eta} < \overset{*}{\xi}\,\overset{o}{\eta} \tag{5-15}$$

Two points are made by this relation. Both $\overset{o}{\xi}$ and $\overset{o}{\eta}$ cannot be zero,
nor can both $\overset{*}{\xi}$ and $\overset{*}{\eta}$. This means that the superposition 5-11 or
5-14 always moves the solution away from the breakpoint in the ξ-η
plane. Also, the slope of the line segment produced by superimpos-
ing the unit solution $\overset{*}{z}$ in which $v_b > 0$ must be greater than the slope
of the segment formed with the unit solution $\overset{o}{z}$ in which $x_b > 0$. This
is illustrated in Fig. 5-5. In terms of the electrical model, diode b

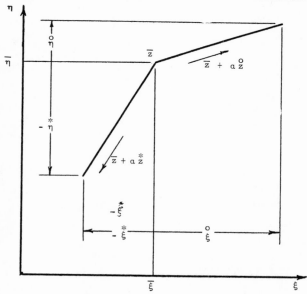

Fig. 5-5 A breakpoint and the superposition of unit solutions

which is at breakpoint for the basic solution $\bar{z}$ shifts to the closed
state when $\overset{o}{z}$ is added to $\bar{z}$, or shifts to the open state when $\overset{*}{z}$ is
added. Naturally the second case produces the greater incremental
resistance, as seen at the ξ-η terminal pair, and causes a greater
slope in the breakpoint curve.

Computing the New Basis Inverse

The basis for the new basic solution 5-13 differs from the previous
one in that the vector P_r appears in the new basis while P_s does not.
The rows of the inverse of the new basis S_i may be calculated from
the rows of the previous inverse $\bar{S}_i$ by means of the formulae

$$
S_i = \begin{cases} \bar{S}_i - \dfrac{\bar{S}_i^T P_r}{\bar{S}_s^T P_r}\, \bar{S}_s\,, & i \ne r \\[2em] \dfrac{1}{\bar{S}_s^T P_r}\, \bar{S}_s\,, & i = r \end{cases}
\qquad (5\text{-}16)
$$

This calculation can always be performed because $\bar{S}_s{}^T P_r$ is always greater than zero. That the S_i formed this way actually are the inverse of the new basis may be verified by multiplying by the vectors of the new basis B :

If $\quad i \ne r$,

$$
S_i{}^T P_j = \bar{S}_i^T P_j - \frac{\bar{S}_i{}^T P_r}{\bar{S}_s{}^T P_r}\, \bar{S}_s{}^T P_j
$$

$$
= S_i{}^T P_j = \begin{cases} 1\,, & i = j \\ 0\,, & i \ne j \end{cases}\,, \quad i \text{ in B}
$$

If $\quad i = r$,

$$
S_r{}^T P_j = \frac{\bar{S}_s{}^T P_j}{\bar{S}_s{}^T P_r} = \begin{cases} 1\,, & j = r \\ 0\,, & j \ne r \end{cases}\,, \quad j \text{ in B}
$$

Tracing the Breakpoint Curve

Suppose that one is interested in tracing the breakpoint curve of a terminal-pair system P and has at hand a basic solution of the system z and the corresponding inverse vectors S_i . Then the steps involved are the following:

Step (1) Two unit incremental solutions are available at the given basic solution. From this pair, select the one which proceeds in the desired direction along the breakpoint curve. The column P_r associated with this unit incremental solution is the first vector to be substituted into the basis.

Step (2) Determine the vector P_s which drops from the basis by applying the rule 5-12. If there is no i corresponding to a vector from P_X or P_V with $S_i^T P_r > 0$, the last breakpoint has been reached and the algorithm terminates.

Step (3) Compute the values of the new basic variables using 5-13, and construct the new vectors of the basis inverse by means of 5-16.

Step (4) The next vector P_r to be substituted in the basis is the conjugate of P_s. Return to Step (2).

These rules, with the exception of Step (4), are identical to the simplex method. The difference lies in the manner of selecting the vector to be substituted in the basis.

The Method in Case of Degeneracy

So far only one diode in the breakpoint state has been allowed for any basic solution. By means of this condition it is insured that there will be a unique vector P_s selected to drop from the basis in each iteration. If this condition is removed, the vector to be dropped may not be uniquely determined by the above rules. An incorrect choice can result in a reversal in the direction of tracing the break-point curve; in the simplex procedure endless cycling can occur. In the case of the simplex method this degeneracy problem was re-solved by Charnes [4] who gave an infallible rule for choosing the vector to leave the basis. A more elegant mathematical treatment of the matter has since been formulated by Wolfe [11]. Using this same formalism, the breakpoint-stepping algorithm is generalized in Appendix H to apply to the degenerate case. There the terminal-pair system is embedded in a larger system in which, in a sense, each basic solution has only one pair of conjugate variables at break-point. It is shown that the quantity corresponding to $\xi + \eta$ increases strictly with each step of the method. The only place where the pro-cedure of the previous paragraph breaks down is in Step (2) where the vector to be dropped from the basis may not be uniquely deter-mined. The development in Appendix H demonstrates that this pro-cedure still works, providing the rule 5-12 for determining the vector to be dropped in Step (2) is modified as follows:

Step (2) i) Compute the quantities

$$a_i = \frac{\overline{z}_i}{S_i^T P_r} \, , \qquad \begin{array}{l} \text{i corresponding to vectors from} \\ P_X \text{ and } P_V \text{ which are in the ba-} \\ \text{sis and have } S_i^T P_r > 0 \end{array}$$

If there are no such vectors, the last breakpoint has been reached. The vector

$$z = \overline{z} + a \overset{o}{z}$$

is then a solution of the terminal-pair system for all positive values of a.

ii) Let $\bar{a}$ have the value of the smallest a_i computed above, and let R be the set of all i such that $a_i = \bar{a}$. If R contains only one member, then P_r is the corresponding vector. Otherwise take j = 1 and proceed.

iii) Evaluate the quantities

$$a_{ij} = \frac{S_{ij}}{S_i^T P_r}$$

for each i in R. Let $\bar{a}_j$ be the smallest of these.

iv) Remove from R all i except those for which $a_{ij} = \bar{a}_j$. If only one member remains in R, the corresponding vector is P_r. Otherwise repeat (iii) with j incremented by one unit. Any ties are always resolved by the time $j = m + n + 1$.

The Method When Q is Null

Although the method developed in the preceding sections will work for any terminal-pair system, the method simplifies sufficiently in certain important special cases to warrant special consideration. First, the case where the matrix O is null will be considered. As was pointed out in Chapter 3 the breakpoint curve will then consist of only horizontal and vertical line segments. The terminal-pair system becomes the uncoupled system

η	x	ξ	y	v	
	A	e			b
		A^T	I		c
1		e^T			0

Consider the properties of a basis for this system. A basis must contain precisely m + n + 1 columns of the system-matrix P (where A has m rows and n columns). However, a basis can contain no more than m linearly independent vectors from $[P_x \ P_\xi]$ because each of these is zero except for the first m components. Similarly, a basis can contain no more than n + 1 vectors from $[P_\eta \ P_y \ P_v]$. It follows that:

Any basis for a terminal-pair system in which O is null must contain exactly m vectors from $[P_x \ P_\xi]$ and exactly n + 1 vectors from $[P_\eta \ P_y \ P_v]$.

Thus such a basis has the form

$$B = \begin{bmatrix} B_P & 0 \\ 0 & B_D \end{bmatrix}$$

It is made up of a <u>primal basis</u> B_P containing m linearly independent columns from

$$[A \quad e]$$

and a <u>dual basis</u> B_D containing $n + 1$ linearly independent columns from

$$\begin{bmatrix} 0 & A^T & I \\ 1 & e^T & 0 \end{bmatrix}$$

The inverse of this basis is obviously

$$\begin{bmatrix} B_P^{-1} & 0 \\ 0 & B_D^{-1} \end{bmatrix}$$

An immediate result of the special structure of the basis inverse concerns the unit solution associated with a nonbasic vector P_r:

$$\overset{o}{z}_i = \begin{cases} -S_i^T P_r & i \text{ in } B \\ 1 & i = r \\ 0 & \text{other } i \end{cases}$$

If P_r is a column of P_X, then $\overset{o}{\eta} = \overset{o}{y} = \overset{o}{v} = 0$; if P_r is a column of P_V , then $\overset{o}{\xi} = \overset{o}{x} = 0$. Therefore on a step of the algorithm in which a column of P_X is substituted in the basis, only ξ and x may change while η , y , and v must remain fixed. For this reason, the vector which drops from the basis must also be a column of P_X. Likewise, on a step in which a column of P_V is introduced, η , y , and v may change, but ξ and x are fixed. The vector dropped must be from P_V. Since the vector introduced on one step is the conjugate of the vector dropped on the previous step, it follows that the algorithm alternately selects the vector to be introduced from P_X and P_V. Furthermore the primal basis B_P stays fixed on a step in which the dual variables η , y , and v are changed while the dual basis remains the same when the primal variables change.

Next it will be shown that it is only necessary to employ one of the inverses B_P^{-1} or B_D^{-1} in the breakpoint tracing computation.

Suppose there is at hand a basic solution $\bar{z} = (\bar{\eta}, \bar{x}, \bar{\xi}, \bar{y}, \bar{v})$ with corresponding basis

$$\bar{B} = \begin{bmatrix} \bar{B}_P & 0 \\ 0 & \bar{B}_D \end{bmatrix}$$

but only the inverse vectors $(\bar{S}_P)_i$ of $\bar{B}_P$. Let $(P_P)_i$, i in $\bar{B}_P$ be the columns of $P_P = [A \; e]$ which are in the primal basis $\bar{B}_P$. Then

$$(S_P)_i^T (P_P)_j = \begin{cases} 1, & i = j \\ 0, & i \neq j \end{cases}, \quad i, j \text{ in } \bar{B}_P$$

Suppose also that the basic solution $\bar{z}$ has been reached by a primal step in which the primal vector $(P_P)_r$ dropped from the basis. Now note that the vector $(P_P)_\xi = e$ is always a member of B_P, and consider the quantities

$$\overset{*}{y} = -(\bar{S}_P)_\xi$$

$$\overset{*}{v} = A^T (S_P)_\xi = -A^T \overset{*}{y}$$

$$\overset{*}{\eta} = e^T (\bar{S}_P)_\xi = -e^T \overset{*}{y}$$

One has

$$\overset{*}{v}_i = -(P_P)_{x_i}^T (\bar{S}_P)_\xi = 0 \qquad \text{if } x_i \text{ is in } \bar{B}_P$$

and

$$\overset{*}{\eta} = (P_P)_\xi^T (\bar{S}_P)_\xi = 1$$

Then it is apparent that $\overset{*}{z} = (\overset{*}{\eta}, 0, 0, \overset{*}{y}, \overset{*}{v})$ is a unit incremental solution of the terminal-pair system.

Since a primal step has just been completed, the unit solution $\overset{*}{z}$ in which all primal variables are zero must be the unit solution to be superimposed on $\bar{z}$ to accomplish the dual step. Since $\overset{*}{\eta} > 0$, $\overset{*}{z}$ should be added to $\bar{z}$ if the breakpoint curve is being traced toward positive ξ and/or η and should be subtracted if the opposite course is being followed. In the former case the dual step of the tracing method is given by the formulae

$$y(\bar{a}) = \bar{y} - \bar{a} (\bar{S}_P)_\xi$$

$$v_i(\bar{a}) = \bar{v}_i, \qquad x_i \text{ in } \bar{B}_P$$

$$v_i(\bar{a}) = \bar{v}_i - \bar{a}(P_P)_{x_i}^{T}(S_P)_\xi\,, \quad x_i \text{ not in } \bar{B}_P$$

$$\eta(\bar{a}) = \bar{\eta} + \bar{a}$$

where

$$\bar{a} = \text{Min}\left[\frac{\bar{v}_i}{(P_P)_{x_i}^{T}(\bar{S}_P)_\xi}\right]$$

$$i \text{ such that } x_i \text{ is not in } \bar{B}_P$$

As presented above, the specialization of the breakpoint-tracing algorithm does not have provision to handle the problem of degeneracy. Unfortunately, the author has been unable to specialize the rule given on page 87 so that the information in the primal basis alone is sufficient to make all of the required decisions.

The method described in this section can also be formulated so as to make use of information contained in the dual basis B_D only.

The Case When Q and b or c Are Null

The second special case of interest is when one of the sets of constants b or c is null as well as O. In the electrical model c being null is equivalent to replacing the voltage sources with short circuits. The resulting system will be called a primal reduced terminal-pair system. It has a breakpoint curve in which all horizontal line segments are coincident with the horizontal axis (Theorem G-3), and therefore must have one of the forms shown in Fig. 5-6. As a

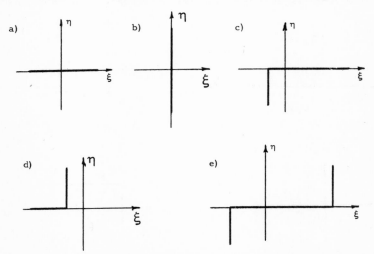

Fig. 5-6 Possible breakpoint curves for a primal reduced terminal-pair system

consequence all breakpoints must lie on the vertical axis. Since this case is a further specialization of the uncoupled system discussed in the previous section, the results obtained there also apply to the present case. In particular, for any basis B of the system, the dual portion B_D must contain exactly $n + 1$ linearly independent columns from

$$
\begin{bmatrix}
0 & A^T & I \\
1 & e^T & 0
\end{bmatrix}
$$

The corresponding basic solution z must be such that

$$
\sum_{i \text{ in } B_D} z_i (P_D)_i = 0
$$

This can only be true if all of the dual variables η, y, and v are zero. This means that the dual step of the tracing method does not change the values of the dual variables at all, but merely indicates which primal vector is to be entered into the basis next.

Similar remarks hold for the dual reduced terminal-pair system in which both O and b are null. In that case, the primal variables x and ξ are zero for any basic solution. If O, b and c are all zero, then the terminal-pair system is completely degenerate and all breakpoints are at the origin of the ξ-η plane. Then the breakpoint curve must have one of the simple forms shown in Fig. 5-7. Note that this is an extremely degenerate case, for all pairs of conjugate variables are at breakpoint for each basic solution.

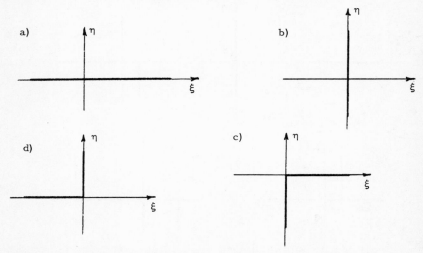

Fig. 5-7 Possible breakpoint curves for a completely degenerate terminal-pair system

Chapter 6

BREAKPOINT TRACING METHODS FOR
GENERAL LINEAR AND QUADRATIC PROGRAMS

The breakpoint stepping procedure developed in Chapter 5 will be
employed here to construct several algorithms for obtaining optimal solutions to general linear and quadratic programs. To accomplish this, electrical network models of the general linear and quadratic programs will be formulated. Terminal-pair systems will be
constructed around these models in such a manner that i) a basic
solution and the vectors of the basis inverse are obvious, and ii)
tracing the resulting breakpoint curve leads to a solution of the network and hence to the optimal vectors of the programming problem
and its dual.

Electrical Models for General Linear and Quadratic Programs

In order to simplify the drawings of networks in which banks of
similar elements appear, the symbols employed in Chapter 5 to
simplify the model of the terminal-pair system will also be used
here. An electrical model of the dual pair of quadratic programs
discussed in Chapter 2 is shown in Fig. 6-1. The primal variables
x and u are represented by currents and the dual variables y and
v by voltages. By inspecting the figure it is evident that any solution of the network model is also a solution of the Lagrangian problem associated with the dual programs.

In correspondence with the physical interpretations given in Chapter 3, the electrical sources represent the constant vectors of the
constraint inequalities, the diodes embody the principle of complementary slackness, and the primal-dual coupling relation appears
as the resistance array P. The conservation of electrical power is
equivalent to the equality of objective functions required by the duality theorem.

The voltage reduced network associated with the model is obtained
by "open circuiting" the resistance array P (setting $x_Q = 0$) and setting the current source values to zero. Its significance, as was mentioned in Chapter 3, is that $(x_Q = 0,\ x_L = 0,\ y_Q,\ y_L)$ is a solution
of the voltage reduced network if and only if $(y_Q,\ y_L)$ is a feasible
vector of the dual programming problem. Similarly, the current
reduced network is obtained by "short circuiting" the resistance
array (setting $y_Q = 0$) and setting the voltage source values to zero,
and it has a solution $(x_Q,\ x_L,\ y_Q = 0,\ y_L = 0)$ if and only if (x_Q, x_L)
is a feasible vector of the primal program.

93

94

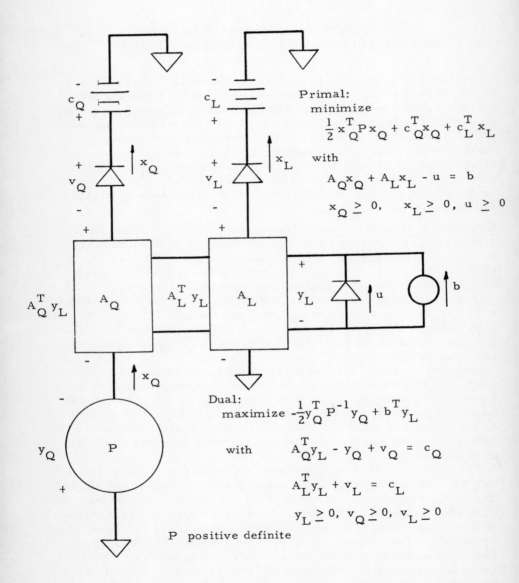

Primal:
minimize

$$\frac{1}{2} x_Q^T P x_Q + c_Q^T x_Q + c_L^T x_L$$

with

$$A_Q x_Q + A_L x_L - u = b$$

$$x_Q \geq 0, \quad x_L \geq 0, \; u \geq 0$$

Dual:
maximize $-\frac{1}{2} y_Q^T P^{-1} y_Q + b^T y_L$

with $\quad A_Q^T y_L - y_Q + v_Q = c_Q$

$$A_L^T y_L + v_L = c_L$$

$$y_L \geq 0, \; v_Q \geq 0, \; v_L \geq 0$$

P positive definite

Fig. 6-1 Electrical model of the dual pair of quadratic programs

Note that for any quadratic program stated in the form given in
Fig. 6-1, the duality principle shows that any method for solving
the primal formulation is in reality two methods, for it could also
be applied to the dual formulation. This is not the case for the
more general quadratic programming formulation stated and modelled in Fig. 6-2. There the primal program yields a Lagrangian
problem which gives the correct conditions for a solution of the network model. However, it is not clear how to construct a dual formu-

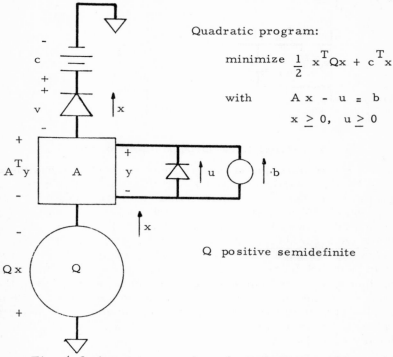

Quadratic program:

$$\text{minimize } \frac{1}{2} x^T Q x + c^T x$$

$$\text{with} \qquad A x - u = b$$

$$x \geq 0, \quad u \geq 0$$

Q positive semidefinite

Fig. 6-2 A more general quadratic programming model

lation for this more general problem. (It is possible by means of
a change of variables to put any quadratic program with a positive
semidefinite objective function into the formulation of Fig. 6-1.
But a neater resolution of the question is to be desired.)

Fig. 6-1 becomes a model of the dual pair of linear programs
when the left side is discarded. A second model of the dual linear
programs is formed by replacing the banks of voltage and current
sources with transformer banks (Fig. 6-3). This produces a model
with just one voltage source and one current source. This device
will enable us to design one algorithm for linear programming which
apparently has no counterpart in quadratic programming.

In the following sections, two types of algorithms for solving the
network models will be discussed. In the first type the sources of

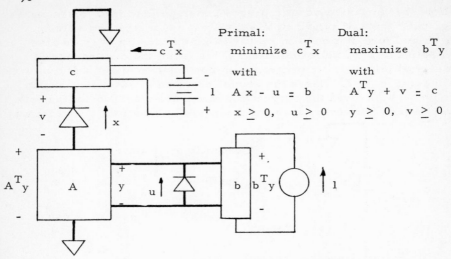

Primal:

minimize $c^T x$

with

$A x - u = b$

$x \geq 0, \quad u \geq 0$

Dual:

maximize $b^T y$

with

$A^T y + v = c$

$y \geq 0, \quad v \geq 0$

Fig. 6-3 Second linear programming model

the network are initially set to zero where the network has the obvious solution of zero current and voltage. The methods proceed by gradually increasing the source value to their assigned levels while keeping the network laws satisfied. It is as if one gradually "turned on the juice" with a potentiometer. They will therefore be called valve algorithms. In the second type the sources are maintained at the assigned values, but the effect of the sources is kept from the network by being shunted through a by-pass. The algorithm then gradually transfers the effect of the sources from the by-pass to the network. These will be called by-pass algorithms. The valve algorithms are based on the second electrical model for the general linear program, and the by-pass algorithms are based on the model of Fig. 6-1.

A Valve Algorithm for Solving the Current Reduced Network

First, the breakpoint tracing method will be applied to determining a solution of the current reduced network associated with the network model of a quadratic or linear program. In programming terminology this is equivalent to forming a feasible vector for the primal constraints

$$A x - u = b$$

$$x \geq 0, \quad u \geq 0$$

$(6-1)$

Consider the terminal-pair system shown in Fig. 6-4. Since the model contains no voltage or current sources, this system is completely degenerate, and all its breakpoints are at the origin of the $\xi - \eta$ plane. Now suppose that the constraint relations 6-1 are

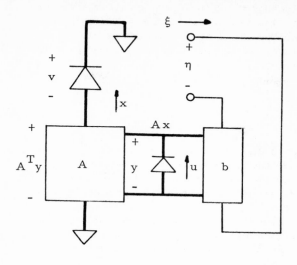

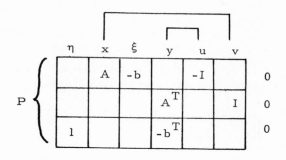

	η	x	ξ	y	u	v	
P			A	-b		-I		0
					A^T		I	0
	1				$-b^T$			0

Fig. 6-4 Valve method for solving the current reduced network

feasible, that is, there is some $(\bar{x}, \bar{u})$ satisfying 6-1 . Then $(\eta = 0,$
$\bar{x}, \xi = 1, y = 0, \bar{u}, v = 0)$ is a solution of the terminal-pair system
with the terminal solution $(\xi = 1, \eta = 0)$. Conversely, if the system
has a terminal solution (1, 0), then the corresponding x and u
form a feasible vector of 6-1 . It follows that:

    The constraint relations 6-1 are feasible if and only if the
    breakpoint curve of the terminal-pair system in Fig. 6-4
    passes through the point (1, 0).

    A convenient basic solution of the terminal-pair system is avail-
able by inspection, namely with the basic variables $\eta = 0, u = 0,$
$v = 0$. With this choice the basis vectors B are the unit vectors of
the $m + n + 1^{th}$ order identity matrix and the basis inverse S likewise consists of unit vectors. Note that the vector P_ξ is not in the

basis as was required by the development in Chapter 5. In all other respects this is a proper basic solution. The one objection will be met by choosing P_ξ as the vector to be substituted into the basis to initiate the breakpoint tracing process. Note that the unit solution

$$\overset{o}{z}_i = \begin{cases} - S_i^T P_\xi, & \text{i in B} \\ 1, & \text{i} = \xi \\ 0, & \text{other i} \end{cases}$$

corresponding to this substitution has $\overset{o}{\xi} = 1$ and therefore automatically starts the tracing in the correct direction along the breakpoint curve. Of course, because of the degenerate nature of the terminal-pair system the generalized procedure given in Chapter 5 must be used.

The tracing process is carried on until Step 2 fails to indicate a vector to be dropped from the basis, and a basic solution $\bar{z} = 0$ and unit solution $\overset{*}{z}$ are available such that

$$z = \bar{z} + a \overset{*}{z} \qquad\qquad (6\text{-}2)$$

is a solution of the system for all $a \geq 0$. There are two possibilities: Since the terminal-pair system is completely degenerate, the ray (6-2) is either the positive ξ-axis or the positive η-axis. If $\overset{*}{\eta} > 0$ the latter case holds, the breakpoint curve does not pass through the point (1, 0), and there is no feasible vector for 6-1. If $\overset{*}{\xi} > 0$, then $(\overset{*}{x}/\overset{*}{\xi}, \overset{*}{u}/\overset{*}{\xi})$ is the desired feasible vector.

Recall that a basis for a system in which Q is null must have the form

$$B = \begin{bmatrix} B_P & O \\ O & B_D \end{bmatrix}$$

As a consequence, the primal basis B_P associated with the basic solution $\bar{z}$ must consist of m linearly independent vectors from the primal vector set

$$[A \quad I]$$

The fact that this primal basis and its inverse S_P^T are available at the conclusion of the tracing process will be utilized in initiating the algorithms described in the following sections.

A By-Pass Algorithm for Solving the Current Reduced Network

A second way of employing the breakpoint tracing technique in solving the current reduced network is illustrated in Fig. 6-5. In this terminal-pair system, T is a diagonal matrix consisting of plus and minus ones such that

99

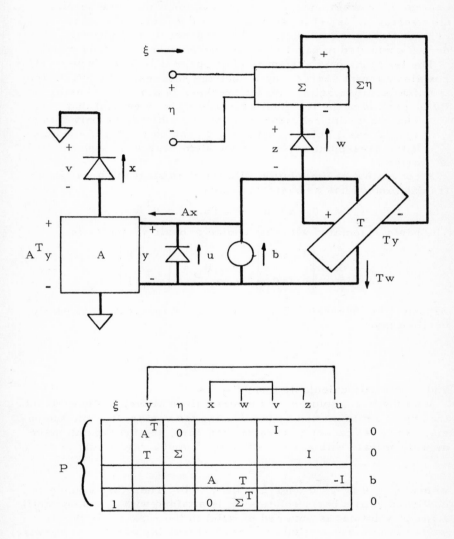

Fig. 6-5 By-pass method for solving the current reduced network

$$T_{ii} = \begin{cases} +1 & \text{if } b_i \geq 0 \\ -1 & \text{if } b_i < 0 \end{cases}$$

In the electrical model, T is represented by a diagonal bank of one-to-one d-c transformers. Each component of the special column vector Σ is +1 so that $\Sigma^T w$ is the sum of the components of w. Here the transformer bank representing Σ has its secondaries connected in parallel since currents are being summed.

The terminal-pair system is of the primal reduced form as it contains current sources but no voltage sources. Therefore its terminal solution set has all its breakpoints along the ξ-axis. By inspection of the terminal-pair system it is evident that:

The constraint relations 6-1 are feasible if and only if the system has a solution with $w = 0$, which is true if and only if the breakpoint curve of the system passes through the origin.

A convenient basic solution with which to start the breakpoint tracing method has as basic variables

$$v = 0, \quad z = 0, \quad w = Tb, \quad \xi = \Sigma^T w$$

The basis associated with this choice of basic variables is

$$B = \begin{bmatrix} I & 0 \\ 0 & B_D \end{bmatrix} \qquad B_D = \begin{bmatrix} T & 0 \\ \Sigma^T & 1 \end{bmatrix}$$

Although the inverse of B_D is not readily apparent, it is easily verified that

$$S_D^T = B_D^{-1} = \begin{bmatrix} T & 0 \\ \Sigma^T T & 1 \end{bmatrix}$$

and is trivially calculable from B_D.

With the basic solution and inverse given above, the breakpoint tracing is set in motion by introducing the vector P_ξ into the basis. Since ξ cannot be greater than zero, the breakpoint curve must terminate with a basic solution $\bar{z}$ and a ray of solutions

$$z = \bar{z} + a z^*$$

where $\bar{\xi} \leq 0$, $\bar{\eta} = 0$ and $\overset{*}{\xi} = 0$, $\overset{*}{\eta} > 0$. Therefore tracing is continued until a basic solution $\bar{z}$ is attained with $\bar{\xi} = 0$, or until a ray of solutions is obtained parallel to the η-axis. In the first case, $\bar{x}$ and $\bar{u}$ constitute the desired feasible vector. Otherwise, the constraints are infeasible.

As in the valve algorithm the final basis contains as its dual portion m linearly independent vectors from

$$[A \quad -I]$$

(If it contained a vector associated with some w_i this could be replaced with the vector associated with u_i.)

Solving the Voltage Reduced Network

Exactly the same techniques as were used in the previous two sections can be employed in solving the voltage reduced network of the linear or quadratic programming model. The mathematical form of the terminal-pair systems for a valve algorithm and a by-pass algorithm are the same as before except for a switch of letters. They are

ξ	y	η	x	v	u	
	A^T	$-c$		I		0
			A		$-I$	0
1			$-c^T$			0

for the valve algorithm and

η	x	ξ	y	z	u	w	v	
	A	0			$-I$			0
	T	Σ				$-I$		0
			A^T	T			I	c
1			0	Σ^T				0

for the by-pass algorithm. Either method will yield a feasible solution (y, v) for the dual constraints

$$A^T y + v = c$$

$$y \geq 0, \quad v \geq 0$$

together with a corresponding basis of n linearly independent vectors from

$$[A^T \quad I]$$

and its inverse.

A Valve Algorithm for Linear Programming

Once a solution (x, u) of the corresponding current reduced network has been found, a complete solution of the linear programming model may be constructed by tracing the breakpoint curve of the terminal-pair system shown in Fig. 6-6. It will be necessary to utilize the partial basis M of m linearly independent vectors from $[A \quad -I]$ and its inverse which are available from the solution of the current reduced network. The terminal-pair system in the figure contains no voltage sources. It is therefore a dual reduced system and all its breakpoints lie on the ξ-axis.

102

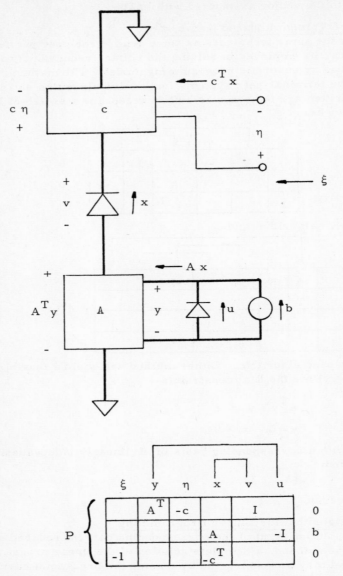

Fig. 6-6 Valve method for completing the solution of
the linear programming model

By considering the figure it is evident that:
    A solution exists for the network model if and only if the
    breakpoint curve contains a point with $\eta = 1$.

As an initial basic solution we may take for the basic variables

$$v = 0, \quad u_i = \bar{u}_i, \quad x_j = \bar{x}_j, \quad \xi = c^T \bar{x},$$

i and j such that P_{u_i} or P_{x_j} is in M. The corresponding basis
is

$$B = \begin{bmatrix} -I & 0 \\ 0 & B_D \end{bmatrix}, \qquad B_D = \begin{bmatrix} M & 0 \\ d^T & 1 \end{bmatrix}$$

where d contains the elements of $\begin{bmatrix} -c \\ 0 \end{bmatrix}$ corresponding to columns of $[A \ -I]$ in M. The inverse of B_D is found to be

$$B_D^{-1} = \begin{bmatrix} M^{-1} & 0 \\ -d^T M^{-1} & 1 \end{bmatrix}$$

The tracing of the breakpoint curve is started by introducing P_η
into the basis. The tracing is terminated when a ray of solutions

$$z = \bar{z} + a \overset{*}{z} \tag{6-3}$$

of the terminal-pair system has been found. If $\overset{*}{\eta} > 0$, (6-3) gives
the solution of the network with $a = 1/\overset{*}{\eta}$. If $\overset{*}{\xi} > 0$, then the network has no solution.

Since the terminal-pair system involved in this method is dual
reduced, the primal step of the tracing procedure does not change
the values of the primal variables (which are all zero), but merely
indicates which vector is to enter the basis on the next dual step.
Tracing the breakpoint curve of this model appears equivalent to
Dantzig's simplex method [9] in that the primal variables x and
v constitute a feasible vector for the primal linear program at
each step and the objective function $\eta = -c^T x$ always decreases
with each iteration. The breakpoint tracing algorithm differs from
the simplex method in that the next primal vector to be entered in
the basis is determined from the dual step. In the simplex method
this vector is selected to give the greatest rate of decrease of the
objective function. Unfortunately the author's method apparently
requires the use of the complete basis for the terminal-pair system
consisting of the primal basis B_P and the dual basis B_D to avoid
problems of degeneracy, while the simplex procedure needs only
the dual basis, and is therefore more efficient in terms of storage
requirements.

In a somewhat similar manner Lemke's dual simplex method
[22] follows the same steps, but only makes use of the primal
inverse B_P^{-1} of the terminal-pair system. The relationship of
these three methods is not completely clear and further study would
seem warranted.

A By-Pass Algorithm for Linear and Quadratic Programming

The terminal-pair system for a by-pass method of solving the quadratic programming network model is shown in Fig. 6-7. To initiate the algorithm it is necessary to have a solution $(\overline{x}, \overline{u})$ of the current reduced network. In the terminal-pair system all elements are present and it therefore has the most general form of breakpoint curve. The elements of the diagonal matrix T are chosen so that

$$T_{ii} = \begin{cases} + 1 & \text{if } (Qx + c)_i \geq 0 \\ - 1 & \text{if } (Qx + c)_i < 0 \end{cases}$$

and the value of d is given by $d = Tx$.

It is evident that:

The model network possesses a solution if and only if the terminal-pair system has a solution with $t = 0$. This is true if and only if there is a point on the breakpoint curve with $\eta = 0$.

The breakpoint tracing procedure is started with the basic solution

$$x = \overline{x}, \quad u = \overline{u}, \quad t = T(Q\overline{x} + c), \quad \eta = -\Sigma^T t$$

From the construction of T, $t \geq 0$, and therefore $\eta \leq 0$. The corresponding basis matrix is

$$B = \begin{bmatrix} A & -I & 0 & 0 \\ T & 0 & 0 & 0 \\ -Q & 0 & T & 0 \\ 0 & 0 & \Sigma^T & 1 \end{bmatrix}$$

The inverse of B is found to be

$$S^T = B^{-1} = \begin{bmatrix} 0 & T & 0 & 0 \\ -I & AT & 0 & 0 \\ 0 & TQT & T & 0 \\ 0 & -\Sigma^T TQT & -\Sigma^T T & 1 \end{bmatrix}$$

The first vector to be substituted into this basis is P_ξ which starts the tracing in the positive direction along the breakpoint curve. The algorithm is terminated when either a basic solution is found for which $t = 0$ and the network has been solved, or when a ray of solutions

$$z = \overline{z} + a\overset{*}{z}$$

has been found with $\overline{\xi} < 0$, $\overset{*}{\eta} > 0$, $\overset{*}{\xi} = 0$, indicating that no solution exists.

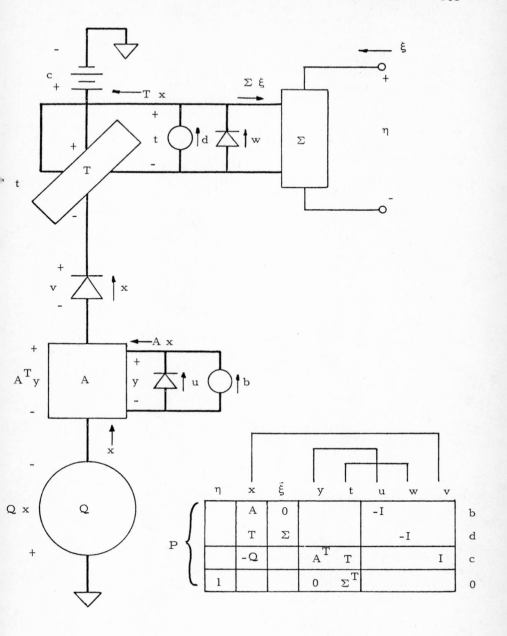

Fig. 6-7 By-pass method for linear and quadratic programming

In application to linear programming this procedure is nearly equivalent to the general primal-dual method of Dantzig, Ford and Fulkerson [10] as applied to the dual linear program. The primal-dual method differs in that dual steps are taken until η attains its highest possible value for the current values of the primal variables. At this point, a primal step is indicated which moves the solution point in the ξ-direction along the breakpoint curve and then the dual steps are resumed. The author's method always alternates between primal and dual steps. In the nondegenerate case, η is always maximized in one step of the primal-dual method, and the two algorithms are identical. Thus they differ only in the way in which degeneracy is handled. In the Ford-Fulkerson method, only information contained in the dual basis inverse B_D^{-1} is needed to avoid the cycles possible in degenerate cases, whereas the by-pass algorithm appears to require knowledge of both B_P and B_D to avoid degeneracy problems. It is evident that the primal-dual algorithm could also be phrased in a form utilizing B_P^{-1} only, and primal steps would be taken until ξ is maximized, whereupon a dual step is indicated which would increase η.

As applied to quadratic programming, the by-pass algorithm is equivalent to a generalization of the method recently developed by Wolfe [29]. Wolfe's method traces the breakpoint curve of the terminal-pair system of Fig. 6-7 by successively superimposing unit incremental solutions which increase η until no further such unit solution can be found. Thus the method will terminate when it reaches any horizontal segment of the breakpoint curve. As a consequence, it is only applicable in the form stated by Wolfe to problems where the breakpoint curve has no horizontal segment, except at the solution point $\eta = 0$. This can be guaranteed only if Q is positive definite. The method could be generalized by employing a dual step as in the primal-dual method whenever η has been maximized but is not yet zero. An obvious variant to this method would be to superimpose unit solutions which increase ξ until it is maximized and follow with a pure primal step to traverse vertical segments of the breakpoint curve. On the other hand, the author's by-pass method avoids all mention of maximization and yields an algorithm in which all steps are executed in the same manner. All three of the methods would take precisely the same steps, at least in the nondegenerate case, while using quite dissimilar decision rules. This discussion shows, moreover, the close relation between Wolfe's method for quadratic programming and the primal-dual method of Dantzig, Ford and Fulkerson.

The quadratic programming procedure proposed by Markowitz [23] can also be interpreted as a scheme for tracing a breakpoint curve. However, the algorithm developed by Frank and Wolfe [16] and a method given by Hildreth [17] do not fit in this category.

The breakpoint tracing method is applicable to the general quadratic programming problem formulation stated at the beginning of
this chapter. However, if the matrix Q has the special form

$$Q = \begin{bmatrix} P & 0 \\ 0 & 0 \end{bmatrix}$$

the problem also has a dual formulation and the method could be
applied to the primal formulation as described above, or to the dual
by starting with a solution of the voltage reduced network. Of course,
in the special case of linear programming the method could always
be used either way.

The reader has probably noticed that the methods of this chapter
have been described in terms of operations on rather large and un-
wieldy matrices. This has been done as an aid in exposition to
show how each procedure can be interpreted as the tracing of the
breakpoint curve of a terminal-pair system. Since the majority
of the elements of the system matrices are zeroes and ones, a practical computer routine would only store the matrices A and Q and
the basis inverse S^T. The effects of the other sections of the system matrix would be coded into the logic of the routine.

Chapter 7

AN APPLICATION OF QUADRATIC PROGRAMMING
TO THE GENERAL PROGRAMMING PROBLEM

In this chapter an iterative method is proposed for obtaining relative optima of the general programming problem formulated in Chapter 2. It is an extension of the gradient methods frequently employed
to compute the unconstrained minimum of a function of many variables
[8]. Specifically it will be shown that the problem of finding the direction of steepest descent for a general programming problem is itself a quadratic programming problem. First, however, let us review gradient methods as applied to unconstrained and equality constrained minimization problems.

Gradient Methods of Minimization

For illustration consider the two variable minimization problem

$$\text{Minimize } \phi\,(x_1,\ x_2)$$

It is desired to find a point in the x_1-x_2 plane for which $\phi(x_1,\ x_2)$
takes on its smallest value. Let $\bar{x}$ in Fig. 7-1 be the point at which
ϕ takes on its minimum. It follows that near $\bar{x}$ the lines along which
ϕ is constant must be closed curves encircling this point. Suppose
that the point x^o is chosen as an initial guess as to the location of the
minimum. A better approximation to the location of the minimum can

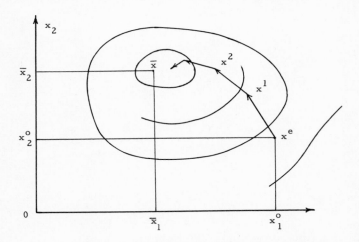

Fig. 7-1 The method of steepest descent

108

be found by moving from the initial point in the direction which yields the greatest rate of decrease in ϕ . This direction, the <u>direction of steepest descent</u>, is directly opposite to the gradient of $\overline{\phi}$ and is perpendicular to the line of constant ϕ passing through the initial point. Thus the new point is given by

$$x^1 = x^o - \lambda \, \partial \phi(x^o) \qquad\qquad (7\text{-}1)$$

where λ is a positive constant. One step in this manner, of course, will not in general take one to the minimum at $\overline{x}$. Hence the gradient step defined by 7-1 should be repeated until some criterion is satisfied indicating that the minimum has been reached. A suitable criterion is that the change in ϕ on the last step be less than some chosen value. The value of the constant λ must be controlled carefully to avoid so large a value that the process does not converge or so small a value that an excessive number of iterations are required. One possible method of controlling λ is by observing the angle θ between succes-sive evaluations of the gradient vector. If this angle becomes too large, λ is decreased; if it is too small, λ is increased. In addition λ is never allowed to be so large that ϕ is increased. Booth [3] gives several variations in which differing means of controlling the step size are employed. The steepest descent technique is applicable to functions of any number of variables, but with the loss of the simple geometric interpretation given above. A flow diagram of the computation is given in Fig. 7-2.

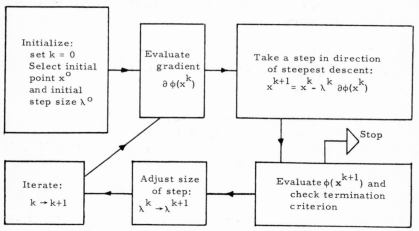

Fig. 7-2 Flow diagram for method of steepest descent

There are several drawbacks to gradient methods of minimization. One is that the method only finds a local minimum of the objective function ϕ . If this function is concave the local minimum will also be a global minimum as pointed out in Chapter 2. Otherwise the ini-tial point x^o must be chosen so that the "nearest" relative minimum is the desired solution. A second difficulty is that the method is not invariant with respect to a change in scale of the variables. If the scale or metric is poorly chosen the method may converge to the minimum at a very slow rate. Criteria for choosing a good metric have been discussed by Crockett and Chernoff [7] and by Feder [13].

Minimization in the Presence of Equality Constraints

The gradient technique may be extended to problems in which the variables must satisfy equality or inequality constraints by modifying the notion of the direction of steepest descent.

A vector u will be called an allowable direction at a point x in the constraint set of a general programming problem, if it is possible to move a small distance away from x in the direction u without leaving the constraint set. For a general programming problem the direction of steepest descent at a point x in the constraint set is the direction, among all allowable directions, for which the rate of decrease of φ is greatest.

First the case of equality constraints will be considered.

Equality constrained minimization problem:

Minimize $\phi(x)$

with $g(x) = 0$

Suppose $\overline{x}$ is a point in the constraint set obtained at some point in the iterative procedure. Let the negative gradient of the objective function be represented by

$$t = - \partial \phi (\overline{x})$$

and let A_i be the gradient of the ith constraint function

$$A_i = \partial g_i (\overline{x})$$

This is a vector normal to the tangent plane of the constraint surface at $\overline{x}$. Then a vector u will be allowable if it lies in the tangent plane to each of the constraint surfaces at $\overline{x}$. This will be true if u is orthogonal to the normal vector of each constraint surface at $\overline{x}$.

$$A_i^T u = 0 \qquad\qquad\qquad (7-2)$$

The direction of steepest descent is then given by the allowable vector of unit magnitude which has the greatest component along the negative gradient of φ. Thus the problem of finding the direction of steepest descent is

Maximize $t^T u$

with $u^T u = 1$

$A^T u = 0$

Employing multipliers v and $-\delta/2$, the Lagrangian expression for this problem is

$$\psi(u, v, \lambda) = t^T u + v^T A^T u - \delta/2\, u^T u$$

The corresponding Lagrangian problem is found by differentiation to be

Find u, v, and δ such that

$$u^T u = 1 \tag{7-3a}$$

$$A^T u = 0 \tag{7-3b}$$

$$t + A v - \delta u = 0 \tag{7-3c}$$

This system of relations can be solved by substituting 7-3c in 7-3b to obtain

$$-\frac{1}{\delta} A^T A v = \frac{1}{\delta} A^T t$$

or

$$v = -M^{-1} A^T t$$

where $M = A^T A$. Finally

$$u = \frac{1}{\delta}\left[I - A M^{-1} A^T \right] t \tag{7-4}$$

The matrix M is positive semidefinite because

$$x^T M x = x^T A^T A x$$

$$= [A x, A x] \geq 0, \quad \text{all } x$$

If the columns of A are linearly independent, M is positive definite and the inverse M^{-1} can be computed and a unique δu obtained. If the columns of A are linearly dependent, one of the normal vectors is a linear combination of the others and the corresponding constraint is redundant at $\bar{x}$. The multiplier δ in 7-4 must be chosen so that the magnitude of u is unity and 7-3a is satisfied.

A flow diagram for minimizing a function subject to equality constraints is shown in Fig. 7-3. Besides the difficulties mentioned in connection with the unconstrained case, there is the problem of keeping the constraints satisfied. The fact that the direction of movement satisfies 7-2 only guarantees that the constraints are not violated for an infinitesmal motion on the direction of steepest descent, whereas finite size steps will actually be taken. Hence it is necessary to provide a block in the flow diagram which moves the point back into

112

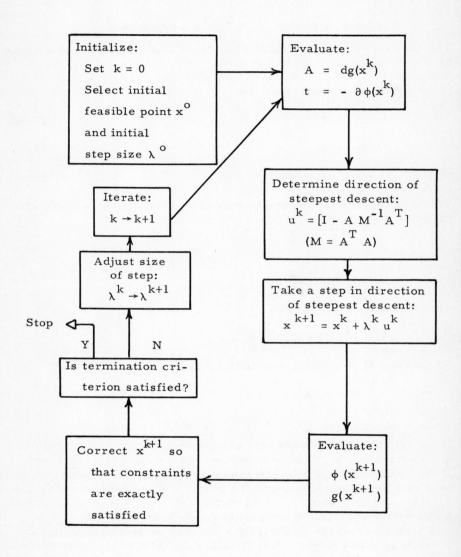

Fig. 7-3 The method of steepest descent with
equality constraints

the constraint surfaces. Also there is the problem of determining the initial point x^0 in the constraint set. These problems will not be discussed further here.

The Direction of Steepest Descent with Inequality Constraints

In the case of inequality constraints a feasible point $\bar{x}$ does not necessarily lie in any particular constraint surface. If $\bar{x}$ does not lie in a constraint surface $g_i(x) = 0$, then this constraint has no effect on the direction of steepest descent at $\bar{x}$. On the other hand, if $g_i(\bar{x}) = 0$, the direction of steepest descent may lie in the constraint surface or it may point into the interior of the constraint set. In order to be an allowable direction of motion away from $\bar{x}$, u must not have a negative component along the normal to any constraint surface which contains $\bar{x}$. The direction of steepest descent is again the unit vector in an allowable direction which has the greatest component along the negative gradient of ϕ. If I is the set of constraint relations which are equality satisfied at the point $\bar{x}$, the direction of steepest descent is given by the programming problem

Maximize $\quad t^T u \qquad\qquad\qquad\qquad\qquad\qquad$ (7-4a)

with $\qquad\quad u^T u = 1 \qquad\qquad\qquad\qquad\qquad$ (7-4b)

$\qquad\qquad A_i^T u \geq 0, \quad i \text{ in } I \qquad\qquad\qquad$ (7-4c)

This is illustrated in Fig. 7-4 for the case of three dimensions. Because of the non-linear equality constraint 7-4b, this program does

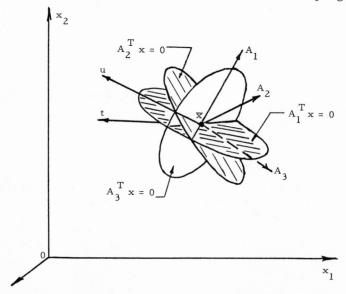

Fig. 7-4 The direction of steepest descent for
three variables

not have a convex constraint set, and the development in Chapter 2 does not guarantee that a relative minimum is a global minimum. In the next section this problem will be shown equivalent to a quadratic program which has a unique solution.

Equivalence with a Quadratic Program

The Lagrangian problem associated with the program 7-4 is, using the results given in Chapter 2,

Find v, u, z, and δ such that

$$\overline{A} v - \delta u + t = 0 \tag{7-5a}$$

$$u^T u = 1 \tag{7-5b}$$

$$\overline{A}^T u \geq 0, \qquad v \geq 0 \tag{7-5c}$$

$$v^T \overline{A}^T u = 0 \tag{7-5d}$$

where $\overline{A}$ is the matrix consisting of those columns of A corresponding to equality satisfied constraint surfaces.

This statement may be simplified if 7-5a is solved to yield

$$\delta u = t + \overline{A} v$$

and the result substituted in 7-5c. Then the Lagrangian problem becomes, for $\delta > 0$,

Find v, z such that

$$- M v + z = \overline{A}^T t \tag{7-6a}$$

$$z \geq 0, \quad v \geq 0 \tag{7-6b}$$

$$z^T v = 0$$

where $M = \overline{A}^T \overline{A}$.

Now 7-6 is exactly the Lagrangian problem associated with the following quadratic program.

Maximize $\frac{1}{2} v^T M v + t^T \overline{A} v$

subject to $v \geq 0$ \hfill (7-7)

As was shown previously, M is a positive definite matrix if the columns of $\overline{A}$ are linearly independent. For this reason the objective function is always bounded from below. Since the constraint set of the quadratic program is obviously feasible, the theory of quadratic programming (Theorem D-4) shows that 7-7 always has a unique optimal solution.

Next we will show that if $(\overline{v}, \overline{z})$ is a solution of 7-5 with $t^T \overline{u} > 0$, then no other allowable unit vector u has as great a component along t, that is,

$$t^T u < t^T \overline{u}$$

for all u not equal to $\overline{u}$ such that

$$u^T u = 1 \quad \text{and} \quad \overline{A}^T u + z = 0, \quad z \geq 0 \quad (7\text{-}8)$$

From relations 7-5 we have

$$\overline{\delta} \, \overline{u}^T \overline{u} - t^T \overline{u} = \overline{u}^T \overline{A} \, \overline{v}$$

$$\overline{v}^T \overline{A}^T \overline{u} = 0$$

and therefore, since $\overline{u}^T \overline{u} = 1$,

$$\overline{\delta} = t^T \overline{u} > 0$$

Let u be any vector not equal to $\overline{u}$ and satisfying 7-8. Then from 7-5a

$$\overline{\delta} \, u^T \overline{u} = t^T u + u^T \overline{A} \, \overline{v}$$

$$\overline{v} \, \overline{A}^T u = \overline{v}^T z \geq 0$$

and therefore

$$t^T u = (t^T \overline{u}) (u^T \overline{u}) - \overline{v}^T z$$

Since u and $\overline{u}$ are not identical, $u^T \overline{u}$ must be less than 1, and it follows that $t^T u < t^T \overline{u}$.

From this discussion it is seen that if 7-5 has a solution $(\overline{\delta}, \overline{u}, \overline{v})$ with $\overline{\delta} = t^T \overline{u} > 0$, then u is the direction of steepest descent. But then $\overline{v}$ and $\overline{z} = \overline{A} t + M \overline{v}$ form a solution of 7-6. It follows that $\overline{v}$ is the unique optimal solution of the quadratic program 7-7. Conversely, if $\overline{v}$ is the optimal solution of 7-7 and

$$\overline{\delta} = t^T t + t^T \overline{A} \, \overline{v} > 0$$

then $\overline{v}, \overline{u} = \dfrac{t + \overline{A} \, \overline{v}}{\overline{\delta}}$ and $\overline{\delta}$ form a solution of 7-5 with $t^T u > 0$.

Therefore we have the following principle:

If the optimal vector $(\overline{v}, \overline{z})$ of the quadratic program has $t^T t + t^T \overline{A} \, \overline{v} > 0$, then the vector $u = t + \overline{A} \, \overline{v}$ is in the direction of steepest descent for the general programming problem at $\overline{x}$. If the optimal vector of the quadratic program has $t^T t + t^T \overline{A} \, \overline{v} \leq 0$, then $\overline{x}$ is a local minimum of the general program.

This result relating to the direction of steepest descent for a general programming problem has also been discovered independently by Zoutendijk [30].

A flow diagram which employs this principle to find a relative optimum for a general programming problem is given in Fig. 7-5. The computation is similar to the equality constraint case except that it is necessary to obtain the optimal vector of a quadratic program in

116

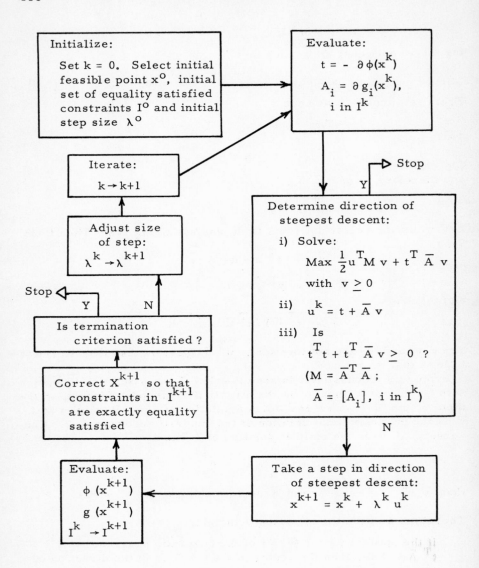

Fig. 7-5 The method of steepest descent with inequality
constraints

each step. The parameters of the quadratic program will not change greatly from one step to the next, and the solution from the previous step will be an excellent starting point for obtaining the new direction of steepest descent. If a quadratic programming algorithm is employed which takes advantage of this fact, the amount of computation required to determine the new direction of steepest descent should be quite small.

Other proposals of procedures for solving general programming problems have appeared in the literature, notably the work of Arrow and Hurwicz [1] and the suggestions of Klein [20]. The former authors transform the original nonlinear program into a saddle-point problem and employ a gradient method to locate the saddle point. Klein's proposal involves the addition of squared "slack" variables to convert the inequalities into equality constraints. A procedure for solving equality-constrained problems may then be used. In each of these methods additional variables are introduced which would certainly slow the process considerably and would increase the chance that an excessive number of iterations might be required. Also, neither of these proposals when applied to a linear program could take advantage of its simplicity.

The method outlined in this chapter, on the other hand, is a direct approach and does not introduce extraneous variables. Applied to a linear program, the number of iterations required would approximate the number of steps taken by the simplex method for the same problem. Applied to a general program, the method would be able to take advantage of any near linearity present in the constraints and objective function. Thus the direct steepest descent approach would appear to offer an efficient and straightforward means of attacking the general programming problem.

Appendix A

Geometrical Elements in Euclidian Space

In this section, geometric concepts are presented which will be used in interpretation of algebraic developments, especially in Appendix B.

Definition: The Euclidian space of n dimensions is the set R^n of all n-tuples of real numbers. An element of R^n may be thought of as a point whose coordinates are the n real numbers or as a vector emanating from the origin whose components along the coordinate axes are the n real numbers. A point or vector x in R^n will be represented by the column matrix

$$x = \begin{bmatrix} x_1 \\ x_2 \\ \cdot \\ \cdot \\ \cdot \\ x_n \end{bmatrix}$$

We will say that a vector y in R^n is greater than a vector x in R^n, and write $y > x$ if each component of y is greater than the corresponding components of x , that is,

$$y > x \text{ implies } y_i > x_i, \qquad i = 1, 2, \ldots, n$$

Similarly we will write $y \geq x$ if the relation holds for each component;

$$y \geq x \text{ implies } y_i \geq x_i, \qquad i = 1, 2, \ldots, n$$

Two vectors x and y are orthogonal if their dot product

$$x^T y = \sum_{i=1}^{n} x_i y_i$$

is equal to zero.

We will have occasion to consider the product of an m-by-n matrix A^T by a vector y. Geometrically this product is to be interpreted as the column vector whose components are the dot products of y with the corresponding columns of A.

$$A^T y = \begin{bmatrix} A_1^T y \\ A_2^T y \\ -\ - \\ A_n^T y \end{bmatrix}$$

On the other hand, if we are concerned with the product of an n-by-m matrix A and a vector x having m components, we can visualize this in R^n as the vector sum of the columns of A each weighted by the corresponding component of x.

$$Ax = x_1 A_1 = x_2 A_2 + \dots + x_m A_m$$

Both of these interpretations will be useful in subsequent proofs.

Definition: A line in R^n is a set of all points x that satisfy a relation

$$\frac{x_1 - a_1}{b_1} = \frac{x_2 - a_2}{b_2} = \dots = \frac{x_n - a_n}{b_n}$$

where a and b are members of R^n. The line includes the point a and is parallel to the direction vector b.

Definition: A hyperplane in R^n is a set of all points x in R^n that satisfy a relation

$$a^T x = \beta$$

where a, a member of R^n, is the normal vector of the hyperplane and β is scalar.

Note that a hyperplane $a^T x = 0$ contains the origin and is the union (the set of all points in any) of all lines containing the origin whose direction vectors are orthogonal to a.

Definition: A half-space in R^n is the set of all points x that satisfy a relation

$$a^T x \geq \beta$$

where a is a member of R^n and β is a scalar. The hyperplane $a^T x = \beta$ is called the bounding hyperplane of the half-space.

It is reasonable to call such a set a half-space, because for each point x strictly on one side of the bounding hyperplane, $a^T x < \beta$, we can produce an image point y strictly on the other side

$$y = x - 2 \frac{a^T x - \beta}{|a|} \frac{a}{|a|}$$

$$a^T y = a^T x - 2a^T x + 2\beta$$

$$= \beta - (a^T x - \beta) \quad \text{so that} \quad a^T y > \beta$$

and this is a one-to-one correspondence between x and y.

Definition: A ray or half-line in R^n is a set containing all points x such that

$$x = a + \lambda b$$

for some $\lambda \geq 0$. Here a and b are fixed members of R^n.

Definition: A cone is a set of points in R^n such that if x is in the set, then

$$y = \lambda x$$

is also in the set for any nonnegative number λ.

Note that by this definition a cone always has its apex at the origin.

Definition: A convex set in R^n is one in which, given any two points, x and y in the set, all points on the line segment joining x and y are also in the set, that is

$$z = (1 - a)x + ay$$

is in the set for any number a between zero and one. The convex hull of a given set is the "smallest" convex set containing the given set. More precisely, it is the intersection of (all points common to) all convex sets which contain the given set. An extreme point of a convex set is a point in the convex set which does not lie on a line segment joining two distinct points of the set.

A polyhedron is a convex set. It is the convex hull of its extreme points which are its vertices.

Definition: A convex polyhedral set in R^n is the intersection of a finite number of half-spaces. It is thus the set of points x which satisfy the relations

$$A_1^T x \geq b_1$$
$$A_2^T x \geq b_2$$
$$- - -$$
$$A_m^T x \geq b_m$$

or

$$A^T x \geq b$$

where A is the n-by-m matrix whose columns are $A_1, \ldots, A_m$, and b is the m-component column vector

$$\begin{bmatrix} b_1 \\ \cdot \\ \cdot \\ b_m \end{bmatrix}$$

In particular, the set of points x which satisfy the constraints of a linear program is a convex polyhedral set. A convex polyhedral set may contain points at an arbitrarily large distance from the origin, that is, it may not be bounded. This is why the term polyhedron is not used for such a set.

In order to justify the above definition we should show that any such set is actually convex.

Proposition: A convex polyhedral set is convex.

Proof: Suppose x and y are points in a convex polyhedral set. Then we have

$$A^T x \geq b$$

$$A^T y \geq b$$

Consider the point on the line segment joining x and y.

$$z = (1 - a)x + ay$$

We have

$$A^T z = (1 - a)A^T x + a A^T y$$

$$\geq (1 - a)b + ab = b$$

$$A^T z \geq b$$

Thus z is also in the convex polyhedral set, and the set is therefore convex.

Definition: A convex polyhedral cone is the intersection of a finite number of half-spaces whose bounding hyperplanes contain the origin. It is the set of points x which satisfy a relation of the form

$$A^T x \geq 0$$

Any convex polyhedral cone is a convex polyhedral set, and hence is convex. We must show, however, that such a set is really a cone.

Proposition: A convex polyhedral cone is a cone.

Proof: Suppose x is a point of a convex polyhedral cone. Then

$$A^T x \geq 0$$

But then

$$A^T(\lambda x) = \lambda A^T x \geq 0$$

for all $\lambda \geq 0$. Thus it is a cone.

An important theorem of convex geometry demonstrates the equivalence of the above definition and a second definition of a convex polyhedral cone which we give now.

Definition: A convex polyhedral cone is the convex hull of a finite number of rays which emanate from the origin. If $A_1, A_2, \ldots, A_m$ are vectors having the direction of the rays, then the cone is precisely all positive linear combinations of these vectors, that is all points

$$z = A x$$

where $x \geq 0$.

That any convex polyhedral cone in a three-dimensional space is consistent with both of these definitions is fairly obvious. In higher dimensional spaces, though the statement is correct, it is moderately difficult to prove. Since these geometric ideas will be used for illustration only, they are not essential to the rigor of the proofs and we will not give the proof of equivalence here.

Appendix B

A Fundamental Theorem on Linear Inequalities*

In the following, a famous theorem on homogeneous linear inequalities is proved which is the basis for the fundamental theorem of the general programming problem. The theorem asserts that there exist vectors x and y which satisfy the system of relations

$$A^T y \geq 0 \qquad\qquad\qquad (B-1a)$$

$$A x = 0 \qquad\qquad\qquad (B-1b)$$

$$x \geq 0 \qquad\qquad\qquad (B-1c)$$

$$A_1^T y + x_1 > 0 \qquad\qquad\qquad (B-1d)$$

where A is an arbitrary m-by-n matrix.

It is easy to show that there are two mutually exclusive cases for this system:

Property B-1: Any solution (x, y) of the system B-1 is such that either

1) $\quad A_1^T y = 0 , \qquad x_1 > 0$

or

2) $\quad A_1^T y > 0 , \qquad x_1 = 0$

Proof: From B-1a and B-1b

$$A_i^T y \geq 0 , \quad \text{all i}$$

$$x_i \geq 0 , \quad \text{all i}$$

Therefore each term of the sum

$$\sum_i x_i A_i^T y \qquad\qquad\qquad (B-2)$$

is nonnegative. But

$$\sum_i x_i A_i^T y = x^T A^T y = y^T (Ax) = 0$$

where the fact has been used that the transpose of a matrix product is the product of the transposes in reverse order. Hence each term of B-2 must be zero. In particular

$$x_1 A_1^T y = 0$$

*The development here is based on a proof of David Gale as given by Tucker [27].

This requires that one of x_1 and A_1^T be equal to zero. Relation B-1d prohibits both being zero simultaneously. Thus the only possibilities are those stated above.

With this property, a nice geometrical interpretation of the theorem may be given. First write the system **B-1** in the expanded form

$$A_1^T y \geq 0 \qquad\qquad 0 = x_1 A_1 + x_2 A_2 + \ldots + x_m A_m \qquad (B\text{-}1b)$$

$$A_2^T y \geq 0 \qquad\qquad x_i \geq 0 \qquad\qquad\qquad\qquad\qquad (B\text{-}1c)$$

$$(B\text{-}1a)$$

$$- \quad - \quad -$$

$$A_m^T y \geq 0 \qquad\qquad A_1^T y + x_1 > 0 \qquad\qquad\qquad (B\text{-}1d)$$

in line with the two interpretations for the product of a matrix and a vector given in Appendix A. Then B-1a requires a hyperplane with normal vector y such that each A_i is either in the hyperplane or has a positive component along the normal vector y. Hence no point of the cone spanned by the A_i's can have a component along y of less than zero. The relations B-1b and B-1c require that the origin be expressed as a positive linear combination of the A_i's. Clearly these demands may be met for any matrix A by choosing $x = 0$, $y = 0$. Thus the relation B-1d is what makes the theorem interesting and significant.

The geometric statement of the theorem is:

Given a set of vectors A_2, A_3, ..., A_m and a single vector $- A_1$, either

1) There exists a hyperplane which separates $- A_1$ from the cone determined by A_2, A_3,..., A_m; specifically, there exists a hyperplane such that $- A_1$ is strictly on one side and all points of the cone are in or to the other side of the hyperplane.

or

2) The vector $- A_1$ is an element of the cone determined by A_2, A_3, ..., A_m.

This interpretation of the theorem is depicted in Fig. B-1.

<u>Theorem B-1</u>: The system of relations

$$A^T y \geq 0, \quad Ax = 0, \quad x \geq 0, \quad A_1^T y + x_1 > 0$$

possesses a solution.

<u>Proof</u>: According to the property proved above, any solution to the system must have either 1) $A_1^T y = 0$, $x_1 > 0$ or 2) $A_1^T y > 0$, $x_1 = 0$. Note that in the first case, if $(x, y) = (\bar{x}, \bar{y})$ is a solution with the required property, then $(x, y) = (\bar{x}, 0)$ also is. Similarly for the second case, if $(\bar{x}, \bar{y})$ is a solution, so is $(0, \bar{y})$. Our proof will demonstrate the existence of a solution having one of these two forms.

a)

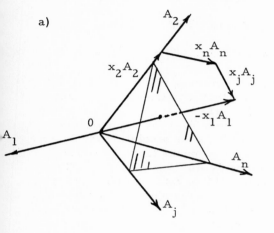

Either $-A_1$ is a positive linear combination of $A_2, \ldots, A_n$

$$-A_1 = \frac{x_2 A_2 + \ldots + x_n A_n}{x_1}$$

$$x_1 > 0,$$

that is, $-A_1$ is in the cone spanned by $A_2, \ldots, A_n$,

b)

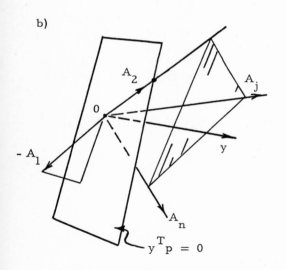

or, there is a hyperplane $p^T y = 0$ such that $A_2, \ldots, A_n$ are all in it or to one side of it, and $-A_1$ is strictly on the other side.

Fig. B-1   Illustrating the statement of Theorem B-1

The proof is by induction on the number m of columns in the matrix A.

A) We first consider the case where A contains one column. Then either

   1) $A_1 = 0$ and $(\overline{y} = 0,\ \overline{x} = 1)$

is a suitable solution, or

   2) $A_1 \neq 0$ and $(\overline{y} = A_1,\ \overline{x} = 0)$

is a suitable solution.

B) Next we assume that the theorem is true for a matrix A of m columns and demonstrate that it is true for a matrix $\overline{A} = [A,\ A_{m+1}]$ of $m+1$ columns.

   1) Suppose we have a solution $(0, x)$ for the matrix A. Then the same solution with $x_{m+1} = 0$ is a solution for $\overline{A}$. Geometrically the solution $(0, x)$ for A means that $-A_1$ is contained in the convex cone determined by A_2, A_3, ..., A_m. Clearly if the cone is enlarged by the addition of an extra member to the set of generating rays, $-A_1$ will still be a member of the new cone.

   2) Suppose we have a solution $(\overline{y},\ 0)$ for the matrix A. Here there are two cases to consider.

   a) Suppose $A_{m+1}^T \geq 0$. Then $(\overline{y},\ 0)$ is still a suitable solution.

In this case we are given a hyperplane with normal vector $\overline{y}$ which separates $-A_1$ from the cone determined by the other columns of A. The new vector A_{m+1} is on the same side of the hyperplane as the cone, hence the same hyperplane will serve to separate $-A_1$ from the cone defined by the enlarged set of rays.

   b) Suppose $A_{m+1}^T < 0$. In this case a solution for $\overline{A}$ cannot be constructed from the solution $(y, 0)$ for A. We proceed by forming the matrix

$$B = [A_1 + \lambda_1 A_{m+1},\ A_2 + \lambda_2 A_{m+1},\ \ldots,\ A_m + \lambda_m A_{m+1}]$$

$$= [B_1,\ B_2,\ \ldots,\ B_m]$$

where

$$\lambda_j = -\frac{A_j^T y}{A_{m+1}^T y} \geq 0$$

This matrix has the property that

$$B_j^T y = A_j^T y + \lambda_j A_{m+1}^T y$$

$$= A_j^T y - A_j^T y = 0$$

Thus the vectors B_j lie in the hyperplane with normal vector y. This situation is illustrated in Fig. B-2a. Each B_j is obtained from the corresponding A_j by adding sufficient amount of the vector A_{m+1} to place the result in the hyperplane.

Since B is a matrix of m columns, and for the induction we have assumed the theorem valid for such a matrix, we are assured of the existence of two vectors v and u such that

$$B^T v \geq 0 \qquad Bu = 0 \qquad u \geq 0 \qquad B_1^T v + u_1 > 0$$

We may take the solution for B to have one of the two forms:

1) $B_1^T v = 0$, $u_1 > 0$ and $(0, u)$ is also a solution
2) $B_1^T v > 0$, $u = 0$ and $(v, 0)$ is also a solution

i) Suppose $(0, u)$ is a solution for B with $u_1 < 0$. We show that

$$[\bar{y} = 0, \quad \bar{x} = (u, \sum_j \lambda_j u_j)]$$

is a solution for A. Certainly

$$\bar{A}^T \bar{y} \geq 0$$

$$\bar{x} \geq 0 \quad \text{because} \quad u \geq 0, \ \lambda \geq 0$$

$$A_1^T y = 0$$

and

$$x_1 = u_1 > 0$$

Now

$$\bar{A}\,\bar{x} = \bar{x}_1 A_1 + \bar{x}_2 A_2 + \ldots + \bar{x}_m A_m + \bar{x}_{m+1} A_{m+1}$$

$$= u_1 A_1 + u_2 A_2 + \ldots + u_m A_m + \sum_j \lambda_j u_j A_{m+1}$$

$$= u_1(A_1 + \lambda_1 A_{m+1}) + u_2(A_2 + \lambda_2 A_{m+1}) + \ldots$$

$$+ u_m(A_m + \lambda_m A_{m+1})$$

$$= Bu = 0$$

so that all requirements are satisfied.

The geometry of this case is shown in Fig. B-2a. Here $-B_1$ lies in the cone defined by B_2, B_3, ..., B_m. Hence $-B_1$ may be expressed as a positive linear combination of B_2, B_3, ..., B_m. By summing A_2, A_3, ..., A_m with the same weights and adding a sufficient multiple of A_{m+1} we can express $-A_1$ as a positive linear combination of the other columns of $\bar{A}$. Hence $-A_1$ lies in the cone defined by A_2, A_3, ..., A_{m+1}.

128

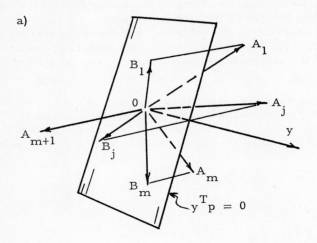

a)

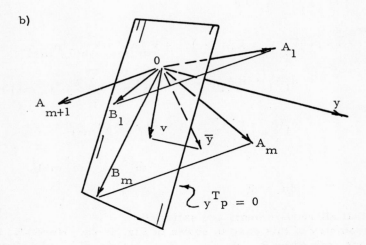

b)

Fig. B-2   Illustrations for proof of Theorem B-1

ii) Finally, suppose $(v, 0)$ is a solution for matrix B with $B_1^T v > 0$.

We show that

$$(\bar{y} = v + \mu y, \quad \bar{x} = 0)$$

where

$$\mu = -\frac{A_{m+1}^T v}{A_{m+1}^T y}$$

is a solution for $\bar{A}$. Note that

$$A_{m+1}^T \bar{y} = A_{m+1}^T v - \frac{A_{m+1}^T v}{A_{m+1}^T y} A_{m+1}^T y = 0$$

Then certainly

$$\bar{A}\,\bar{x} = 0, \quad x \geq 0$$

But

$$A_j^T \bar{y} = A_j^T \bar{y} + \lambda_j A_{m+1}^T \bar{y} = B_j^T \bar{y}$$

$$= B_j^T v + \mu B_j^T y = B_j^T v \geq 0$$

$$j = 1, 2, \ldots, m$$

so

$$\bar{A}^T \bar{y} \geq 0$$

Similarly

$$A_1^T \bar{y} = A_1^T \bar{y} + \lambda_1 A_{m+1}^T \bar{y} = B_1^T \bar{y}$$

$$= B_1^T v > 0$$

so

$$A_1^T \bar{y} > 0$$

The last situation is illustrated in Fig. B-2b. There is a hyper-plane with normal vector v which separates the vector $-B_1$ from the cone spanned by B_2, B_3, ..., B_m. With this we can construct a hyperplane which separates $-A_1$ from the cone spanned by A_2, A_3, ..., A_{m+1} as follows: Take as its normal vector $\overline{y}$, the sum of v and a sufficient multiple of y so that the result is orthogonal to A_{m+1}. Then each B_j has the same component along $\overline{y}$ as it had along v because each B_j is orthogonal to y. Also the component of A_j along $\overline{y}$ is the same as the component of B_j along $\overline{y}$. There-fore all of the A_j are on the same side of the hyperplane whose normal vector is $\overline{y}$, A_1 strictly so. Hence the hyperplane sepa-rates the vector $-A_1$ from the cone as required.

Having shown the theorem valid for m=1, and for m+1 if it is true for m, the theorem must hold for all positive integers and the proof is complete.

Appendix C

The Theory of General Programming*

In this section we will consider problems of the form
General Programming Problem:
Minimize

$$\phi(x)$$

subject to

$$g(x) \geq 0 \qquad\qquad\qquad (C-1)$$

$$x \geq 0 \qquad\qquad\qquad (C-2)$$

where x is an n-vector to be determined and $g(x)$ is a transformation from n-space into m-space

$$g(x) = \begin{bmatrix} g_1(x) \\ g_2(x) \\ -\ - \\ g_m(x) \end{bmatrix}$$

It will be assumed that ϕ and g are differentiable.

Definition: The set of points satisfying C-1 and C-2 is called the constraint set of the programming problem.

The constraint set will be identified by the letter C. It is a convex set if each coordinate function g_i is convex:

Lemma C-1: Let C be the set of points which satisfy

$$g(x) \geq 0, \quad x \geq 0$$

Then C is a convex set if the coordinate functions $g_1, g_2, \ldots, g_m$ of g are convex.

Proof: Let $\bar{x}$ and $\overset{o}{x}$ be any two points in C. Let $x = (1-a)\bar{x} + a\overset{o}{x}$, $0 \leq a \leq 1$, be any point on the line segment joining $\bar{x}$ and $\overset{o}{x}$. Obviously $x \geq 0$. Also,

$$g_i(x) = g_i[(1-a)\bar{x} + a\overset{o}{x}] \geq (1-a)g_i(\bar{x}) + ag_i(\overset{o}{x}) \geq 0$$

by the convexity of g_i.

An important question regarding programming problems asks what conditions will guarantee that a local minimum is an optimal solution. A sufficient condition is that the objective function be concave, and that the constraint set be convex as is proved below.

*This development is based on the paper by Kuhn and Tucker [21].

Theorem C-1: If ϕ is a concave function, $g_1, \ldots, g_m$ are convex functions, and $\bar{x}$ minimizes $\phi(x)$ subject to $g(x) \leq 0$, and $x \leq 0$ in some neighborhood of $\bar{x}$, then $\bar{x}$ minimizes $\phi(x)$ in C.

Proof: Suppose $\bar{x}$ does not minimize $\phi(x)$ in C. Then let $\overset{o}{x}$ be some point in C for which $\phi(\overset{o}{x}) < \phi(\bar{x})$. The line segment $x = (1 - a)\bar{x} + a\overset{o}{x}$, $0 \leq a \leq 1$, is entirely contained in C because C is convex. The objective function evaluated on this line segment is

$$\phi(a) = \phi[\,(1 - a)\bar{x} + a\overset{o}{x}\,] \leq (1 - a)\,\phi(\bar{x}) - a\,\phi(\overset{o}{x})$$

Now there is a point on this line segment which is contained in the neighborhood of $\bar{x}$ but is not identical to $\bar{x}$. Let this point be $x = (1 - \delta)\bar{x} + \delta\overset{o}{x}$ where $0 < \delta \leq 1$. Then

$$\phi(x) = \phi[\,(1 - \delta)\bar{x} + \delta\overset{o}{x}\,] \leq (1 - \delta)\,\phi(\bar{x}) + \delta\,\phi(\overset{o}{x})$$

$$= \phi(\bar{x}) - \delta\,[\,\phi(\bar{x}) - \phi(\overset{o}{x})\,]$$

by the concavity of $\phi(x)$. Since $\phi(\overset{o}{x}) < \phi(\bar{x})$, one has

$$\phi(x) < \phi(\bar{x})$$

which contradicts the assumption that $\bar{x}$ is a local minimum. In order to prove the fundamental theorem of nonlinear programming (Theorem C-2) it is necessary to impose a condition on the constraint set: for each boundary point of the constraint set there must exist a smooth curve terminating on that point and lying wholly within the constraint set. After proving the theorem, an example will be given which shows that the condition is necessary. A precise statement of the condition follows:

Definition: A set C of points satisfying a set of constraints

$$g(x) \leq 0, \quad x \leq 0$$

will be said to satisfy the constraint qualification if the following condition is satisfied for each point $\bar{x}$ of C.

Partition the constraints into two groups E and I such that

$$g_E(\bar{x}) = 0, \qquad\qquad g_I(\bar{x}) > 0$$

$$g(x) = \begin{bmatrix} g_E(\bar{x}) \\ g_I(\bar{x}) \end{bmatrix}$$

and the components of $\bar{x}$ into two groups such that

$$\bar{x} = \begin{bmatrix} \bar{x}_P \\ \bar{x}_Z \end{bmatrix} \ , \qquad \bar{x}_P > 0 \ , \qquad \bar{x}_Z = 0$$

Let $\overset{*}{x}$ be any vector such that

$$[dg_E(x), \overset{*}{x}] \geq 0 \ , \qquad \overset{*}{x}_Z \geq 0 \tag{C-3}$$

that is, $\overset{*}{x}$ points inward from the boundary of C. The condition is that for each $\overset{*}{x}$ satisfying C-3 there exists a differentiable curve

$$x = h(a) \ , \qquad 0 \leq a \leq 1$$

such that

$$h(0) = \bar{x}$$

and

$$dh(0) = \lambda \overset{*}{x} \quad \text{for some } \lambda > 0$$

Theorem C-2: (Fundamental Theorem of General Programming)
Consider the general programming problem:
  Minimize

  $\phi(x)$

with

  $g(x) \geq 0$

  $x \geq 0$

in which ϕ and g are differentiable and the constraint set C satisfies the constraint qualification. A necessary condition that $\bar{x}$ be an optimal vector of the general program is the existence of a $\bar{y}$ such that

$$\partial \phi(\bar{x}) - dg(\bar{x})^T \bar{y} \geq 0 \qquad\qquad g(\bar{x}) \geq 0$$

$$\bar{y} \geq 0 \qquad\qquad \bar{x} \geq 0 \tag{C-4}$$

$$\bar{y}^T g(\bar{x}) = 0 \qquad\qquad \bar{x}^T[\phi(\bar{x}) - dg(\bar{x})^T \bar{y}] = 0$$

A sufficient condition that $\bar{x}$ be optimal in a neighborhood N of $\bar{x}$ is the existence of a $\bar{y}$ satisfying C-4 and that ϕ be concave and g convex in N.

Proof: Let $\bar{x}$ be some point in the constraint set C. Partition the constraints and variables so that

$$x = \begin{bmatrix} \bar{x}_P \\ \bar{x}_Z \end{bmatrix} \qquad \begin{matrix} \bar{x}_P > 0 \\ \bar{x}_Z = 0 \end{matrix}$$

and

$$g(x) = \begin{bmatrix} g_E(\bar{x}) \\ g_I(\bar{x}) \end{bmatrix} \qquad \begin{matrix} g_E(\bar{x}) = 0 \\ g_I(\bar{x}) > 0 \end{matrix}$$

Now consider the system of inequalities:

$$\begin{bmatrix} -\partial\phi(x) & dg_E(x)^T & \begin{matrix} 0 \\ I \end{matrix} \end{bmatrix}^T \overset{*}{x} \geq 0 \tag{C-5a}$$

$$\begin{bmatrix} -\partial\phi(\bar{x}) & dg_E(\bar{x})^T & \begin{matrix} 0 \\ I \end{matrix} \end{bmatrix} \begin{bmatrix} \tau \\ u_E \\ v_Z \end{bmatrix} = 0, \quad \begin{bmatrix} \tau \\ u_E \\ v_Z \end{bmatrix} \geq 0, \tag{C-5b}$$

$$[-\partial\phi(\bar{x}), \overset{*}{x}] + \tau > 0 \tag{C-5c}$$

According to Theorem B-1 and Property B-1, either this system possesses a solution for which $\tau > 0$, or it has a solution for which $[\partial\phi(\bar{x}), \overset{*}{x}] < 0$, but not both. If the system C-5 has a solution $(\overset{*}{x}, \tau, u_E, v_Z)$ with $\tau > 0$, then

$$\bar{y} = \begin{bmatrix} u_E/\tau \\ 0 \end{bmatrix}$$

satisfies the conditions of C-4. Conversely, if $\bar{y}$ satisfies C-4 then $[\overset{*}{x} = 0, \tau = 1, u_E = y_E, v_Z = \partial\phi(\bar{x}) - dg(\bar{x})^T \bar{y}]$ is a solution of C-5 with $\tau > 0$.

To demonstrate the necessity assertion of the theorem, suppose that $\bar{x}$ is an optimal vector of the general programming problem. Suppose also that there is no vector y satisfying C-4, and a contradiction will be obtained. It follows from this last assumption that the system C-5 has no solution with $\tau > 0$. By Theorem B-1, it must have a solution with $[\partial \phi(\overline{x}), \overset{*}{x}] < 0$. From C-5a it is seen that $\overset{*}{x}$ satisfies the relations

$$[dg_E(\overline{x}), \overset{*}{x}] \geq 0, \qquad \overset{*}{x}_Z \geq 0$$

Thus the vector $\overset{*}{x}$ points "into" the constraint set. According to the constraint qualification, a differentiable curve $f(a)$ terminating at $\overline{x}$ exists which is contained entirely in C, and for which

$$df(0) = \lambda \overset{*}{x}, \quad \text{for some } \lambda > 0$$

The derivative of ϕ along this curve is then

$$\frac{d\phi}{da}(0) = [\partial \phi(\overline{x}), \lambda \overset{*}{x}] < 0$$

Therefore there are points in any neighborhood of $\overline{x}$ for which $\phi(\overline{x}) < \phi(\overline{x})$ denying that $\overline{x}$ is optimal.

To demonstrate the sufficiency assertion, suppose that $\overline{x}$ is not optimal and it will be shown that no $\overline{y}$ exists satisfying C-4. If $\overline{x}$ is not optimal then there is a distinct $\overset{o}{x}$ in C such that $\phi(\overset{o}{x}) < \phi(\overline{x})$. Under the convexity assumption, the line segment

$$f(a) = (1 - a)\overline{x} + a\overset{o}{x}, \qquad 0 \leq a \leq 1$$

joining $\overset{o}{x}$ and $\overline{x}$ is contained in C. Since ϕ is concave, the derivative of ϕ along this segment evaluated at $\overline{x}$ must be negative

$$\frac{d\phi}{da}(0) = [\partial \phi(x), \overset{*}{x}] < 0$$

where $\overset{*}{x} = \overset{o}{x} - \overline{x}$. Then $\overset{*}{x}$, together with $\tau = 0$, $u_E = 0$, $v_Z = 0$, form a solution of C-5. It follows from Theorem B-1 that C-5 has no solution with $\tau > 0$. Therefore no $\overline{y}$ will satisfy C-4 unless $\overline{x}$ is optimal.

An example of a programming problem which does not satisfy the constraint qualification is the following:

Minimize $\quad - x_1$

with

$$\theta(x) = (1 - x_1)^3 - x_2 \geq 0$$

$$x_1 \geq 0, \qquad x_2 \geq 0$$

It is evident that the optimal solution of the problem is the boundary point $x_1 = 1$, $x_2 = 0$. It is also true that at this point the direction

$$\overset{*}{x} = \begin{bmatrix} 1 \\ 0 \end{bmatrix}$$

satisfies the conditions C-3 but is not directed into the constraint set. It is only in the case of such anomalous "cusps" that the applicability of the above theorem breaks down.

To complete this appendix, we will show that the constraint set determined by a set of linear inequalities always satisfies the constraining qualification.

Theorem C-3: The convex polyhedral set

$$Ax \geq b, \quad x \geq 0$$

always satisfies the constraint qualification.

Proof: Let $\bar{x}$ be any point of the set. Partition the matrices A, b, and the vector x so that

$$A_I \bar{x} > b_I$$

$$A_E \bar{x} = b_E$$

$$\bar{x}_P > 0$$

$$\bar{x}_Z = 0$$

Let x be any vector such that

$$A_E \overset{*}{x} \geq 0$$

$$\overset{*}{x}_Z \geq 0$$

Define the curve $h(a)$ by

$$h(a) = \bar{x} + a\overset{*}{x}$$

Now

$$A_I h(a) = A_I \bar{x} + a A_I \overset{*}{x} \geq b_I$$

137

for all positive α not greater than some $\alpha_1 > 0$, and

$$A_E \, h(\alpha) = A_E \bar{x} + \alpha A_E \overset{*}{x} \geq b_E \quad \text{for all } \alpha \geq 0$$

Also

$$[h(\alpha)]_P = \bar{x}_P + \alpha \overset{*}{x}_P \geq 0$$

for all positive α not greater than some $\alpha_2 > 0$, while

$$[h(\alpha)]_Z = \bar{x}_Z + \alpha \overset{*}{x}_Z \geq 0 \quad \text{for all } \alpha \geq 0$$

Hence $h(\alpha)$ is contained in the constraint set for all α, $0 \leq \alpha \leq \text{Min} \, [\alpha_1, \alpha_2]$. Obviously $dh(0) = \lambda \overset{*}{x}$ for $\lambda = 1$.

Appendix D

The Fundamental Theorems of Quadratic Programming

The development here concerns the following pair of dual quadratic programs.

Primal Quadratic Program

Find an (x_Q, x_L) which

minimizes $\quad \phi(x_Q, x_L) = \frac{1}{2} x_Q^T P x_Q + c_Q^T x_Q + c_L^T x_L$

subject to $\quad A_Q x_Q + A_L x_L \geq b$

$$x_Q \geq 0 \qquad x_L \geq 0$$

Dual Quadratic Program

Find a (y_Q, y_L) which

maximizes $\quad \theta(y_Q, y_L) = -\frac{1}{2} y_Q^T P^{-1} y_Q + b^T y_L$

subject to $\quad A_Q^T y_L - y_Q \leq c_Q$

$$A_L^T y_L \leq c_L$$

y_Q unrestricted, $\qquad y_L \geq 0$

In these formulations P is assumed to be a symmetric positive definite matrix. It follows that P^{-1} always exists and is also a symmetric positive definite matrix.

Note that the primal problem given here does not represent as general a class of quadratic programs as does the formulation given on p. 8. Specifically, only those problems in that formulation for which the matrix Q has the form

$$Q = \begin{bmatrix} P & 0 \\ 0 & 0 \end{bmatrix}$$

are encompassed by the primal formulation given above. The positive definite matrix P may have any order from zero to the order of Q: the former case is that of linear programming; the latter, that in which the objective function is a positive definite quadratic form.

First we will show that the objective functions of these quadratic programs are concave and convex, respectively.

<u>Lemma D-1</u>: The function

$$\phi(x) = x^T Q x + c^T x$$

is concave if and only if Q is positive semidefinite, and is strictly concave if and only if Q is positive definite.

<u>Proof:</u> By direct computation from the definition of a concave function

$$\phi \left[(1 - a) \overset{o}{x} + a\bar{x} \right] =$$

$$(1 - a)^2 \overset{o}{x}^T Q \overset{o}{x} + 2a (1 - a) \overset{o}{x}^T Q \bar{x} + a^2 \bar{x}^T Q \bar{x}$$

$$+ (1 - a) c^T \overset{o}{x} + a c^T \bar{x}$$

$$= (1 - a) \phi(\overset{o}{x}) + a \phi (\bar{x})$$

$$+ a (1 - a) \ (\overset{o}{x} - \bar{x})^T Q(\overset{o}{x} - \bar{x})$$

The last term is greater than or equal to zero for all choices of $\overset{o}{x}$ and $\bar{x}$ if and only if Q is positive semidefinite. This term is greater than zero for all distinct $\overset{o}{x}$ and $\bar{x}$ if and only if Q is positive definite.

As is pointed out in Chapter 2, the quadratic programs stated above are considered duals because each yields the exact same Lagrangian problem, namely:

<u>Quadratic Programming Lagrangian Problem</u>

Find (x_Q, x_L, y_Q, y_L) such that

$$A_Q x_Q + A_L x_L \geq b \qquad \text{primal constraints} \qquad \text{(D-1)}$$

$$x_Q \geq 0 \qquad x_L \geq 0$$

$$A_Q^T y_L - y_Q \leq c_Q$$
$$A_L^T y_L \leq c_L \qquad \text{dual constraints} \qquad \text{(D-2)}$$
$$y_L \geq 0$$

$$x_Q = P^{-1} y_Q \qquad \text{primal-dual coupling} \qquad \text{(D-3)}$$

$$y_L^T (A_Q x_Q + A_L x_L - b) = 0$$
$$x_Q^T (c_Q - A_Q^T y_L + y_Q) = 0 \qquad \begin{matrix} \text{complementary} \\ \text{slackness} \\ \text{conditions} \end{matrix} \qquad \text{(D-4)}$$
$$x_L^T (c_L - A_L^T y_L) = 0$$

140

Since the objective functions of the primal and dual quadratic programs are concave and convex, respectively, the fundamental theorem of nonlinear programming (Theorem C-2) and Theorem C-1 gives the following result.

Theorem D-1: A feasible vector (x_Q, x_L) of the primal quadratic program is an optimal vector if and only if there is a (y_Q, y_L) such that (x_Q, x_L, y_Q, y_L) is a solution of the quadratic programming Lagrangian problem. Likewise, a feasible vector (x_Q, x_L) of the dual quadratic program is optimal if and only if there is an (x_Q, x_L) such that (x_Q, x_L, y_Q, y_L) solves the Lagrangian problem.

Next, two simple properties are demonstrated which will be used in the proofs of the fundamental theorems of quadratic programming.

Property D-1: If (x_Q, x_L) and (y_Q, y_L) are feasible solutions of the primal and dual quadratic programs, then $\phi(x_Q, x_L) \geq \phi(y_Q, y_L)$.

Proof: By multiplying the constraint inequalities of the primal problem by y_L one obtains

$$y_L^T A_Q x_Q + y_L^T A_L x_L \geq b^T y_L$$

Multiplying the constraints of the dual problem by x_Q and x_L, respectively, gives

$$x_Q^T A_Q^T y_L - x_Q^T y_L \leq c_Q^T x_Q$$

$$x_L^T A_L^T y_L \leq c_L^T x_L$$

The difference between the objective functions is

$$\phi(x_Q, x_L) - \theta(y_Q, y_L) =$$

$$\frac{1}{2} x_Q^T P x_Q + c_Q^T x_Q + c_L^T x_L$$

$$+ \frac{1}{2} y_Q^T P^{-1} y_Q - b^T y_L$$

Using the above relations one finds

$$\phi(x_Q, x_L) - \theta(y_Q, y_L) \geq$$

$$\frac{1}{2} x_Q^T P x_Q - x_Q^T y_Q + \frac{1}{2} y_Q^T P^{-1} y_Q$$

$$= \frac{1}{2} (x_Q - P^{-1} y_Q)^T P (x_Q - P^{-1} y_Q)$$

This quantity is a positive definite quadratic form and can never be negative.

Property D-2: If (x_Q, x_L) and (y_Q, y_L) are feasible vectors for the primal and dual quadratic programs, and $\phi(x_Q, x_L) \le \theta(y_Q, y_L)$, then (x_Q, x_L) and (y_Q, y_L) are optimal solutions of the primal and dual problems.

Proof: By Property D-1, $\phi \ge \theta$, so $\phi = \theta$. If (x_Q, x_L) does not give the lowest value of ϕ the feasible vector which does and (y_Q, y_L) would violate Property D-1. The same reasoning applies to (y_Q, y_L).

Theorem D-2: (Duality Theorem) A feasible vector (x_Q, x_L) for the primal program is optimal if and only if there is a feasible vector (y_Q, y_L) for the dual program, such that $\phi(x_Q, x_L) = \theta(y_Q, y_L)$. A feasible vector of the dual is optimal if and only if there is a feasible vector of the primal, such that $\phi(x_Q, x_L) = \theta(y_Q, y_L)$.

Proof: Only the first assertion will be demonstrated here as the proof of the second is essentially the same. In view of Property D-2, the sufficiency of the condition is clear. To show the necessity, suppose (x_Q, x_L) is an optimal vector of the primal quadratic program. Then, by Theorem D-1, there exists a (y_Q, y_L) such that (x_Q, x_L, y_Q, y_L) solves the Lagrangian problem. This (y_Q, y_L) is then a feasible vector of the dual problem. Now consider the difference between the primal and dual objective functions.

$$\phi(x_Q, x_L) - \theta(y_Q, y_L) =$$

$$\frac{1}{2} x_Q^T P x_Q + c_Q^T x_Q + c_L^T x_L$$

$$+ \frac{1}{2} y_Q^T P^{-1} y_Q - b^T y$$

Using the complementary slackness relations D-4 , this becomes

$$\phi - \theta = \frac{1}{2} x_Q - x_Q^T y_Q + \frac{1}{2} y_Q^T P^{-1} y_Q$$

Finally the coupling relation D-3 yields

$$\phi - \theta = 0$$

Theorem D-3: (Existence Theorem) If both primal and dual quadratic programs possess feasible vectors, then both have optimal vectors. If either of the two programs has no feasible vector, then neither has an optimal vector.

Proof: The second assertion will be proved first. Suppose (x_Q, x_L) is a feasible vector of the primal quadratic program. By Theorem D-1, (x_Q, x_L) can be optimal only if there is a (y_Q, y_L) that satisfies the dual restrictions. The same is true for a feasible vector of the dual problem. To show the sufficiency assertion, suppose (x_Q, x_L) and (y_Q, y_L) are feasible solutions of the primal and dual programs. It is sufficient to show that the objective function of the primal problem is bounded from below on any infinite ray in the primal constraint set. Let

$$\begin{bmatrix} x_Q \\ x_L \end{bmatrix} = \begin{bmatrix} \bar{x}_Q \\ \bar{x}_L \end{bmatrix} + \lambda \begin{bmatrix} \overset{*}{x}_Q \\ \overset{*}{x}_L \end{bmatrix}, \quad \lambda \geq 0$$

be any such ray. In order that (x_Q, x_L) be feasible for all nonnegative values of λ we must have

$$A_Q x_Q + A_L x_L = \lambda (A_Q \overset{*}{x}_Q + A_L \overset{*}{x}_L) + A_Q \bar{x}_Q + A_L \bar{x}_L \geq b$$

and

$$x_Q \geq 0, \quad x_L \geq 0$$

for all $\lambda \geq 0$. This is true only if $(\bar{x}_Q, \bar{x}_L)$ is a feasible vector of the primal problem and

$$A_Q \overset{*}{x}_Q + A_L \overset{*}{x}_L \geq 0$$

$$\overset{*}{x}_Q \geq 0, \quad \overset{*}{x}_L \geq 0 \tag{D-5}$$

Now consider the value of the primal objective function on this ray as a function of λ.

$$\phi(\lambda) = \frac{1}{2} \bar{x}_Q^T P \bar{x}_Q + \lambda \bar{x}_Q^T P \overset{*}{x}_Q + \frac{1}{2} \lambda^2 \overset{*}{x}_Q^T P \overset{*}{x}_Q$$

$$+ c_Q^T (\bar{x}_Q + \lambda \overset{*}{x}_Q) + c_L^T (\bar{x}_L + \lambda \overset{*}{x}_L)$$

$$= \phi(\bar{x}_Q, \bar{x}_L) + \lambda^2 \frac{1}{2} \overset{*}{x}_Q{}^T P \overset{*}{x}_Q$$

$$+ \lambda (\bar{x}_Q{}^T P \overset{*}{x}_Q + c_Q{}^T \overset{*}{x}_Q + c_L{}^T \overset{*}{x}_L)$$

$$= \alpha + \beta \lambda + \gamma \lambda^2$$

If any component of $\overset{*}{x}_Q$ is nonzero, the coefficient of λ^2,

$$\gamma = \frac{1}{2} \overset{*}{x}_Q{}^T P \overset{*}{x}_Q$$

will be greater than zero. In this case $\phi(\lambda)$ is certainly bounded from below. On the other hand, if there is a solution of D-5 with $\overset{*}{x}_Q = 0$, $\phi(\lambda)$ would be bounded below on the ray only if

$$\beta = \bar{x}_Q{}^T P \overset{*}{x}_Q + c_Q{}^T \overset{*}{x}_Q + c_L{}^T \overset{*}{x}_L$$

$$= c_L{}^T \overset{*}{x}_L$$

is nonnegative. We will show that this is true. Since (y_Q, y_L) is a feasible solution of the dual problem

$$A_L{}^T y_L \leq c_L, \quad y_L \geq 0$$

Hence

$$\overset{*}{x}_L{}^T A_L{}^T y_L \leq c_L{}^T \overset{*}{x}_L$$

But also, from D-5

$$y_L{}^T A_L \overset{*}{x}_L \geq 0$$

Therefore

$$c_L{}^T \overset{*}{x}_L \geq 0$$

as desired.

Theorem D-4: (Complementary Slackness Principle and Uniqueness) i) If (x_Q, x_L) is an optimal solution of the primal program and (y_Q, y_L) is an optimal solution of the dual program, then (x_Q, x_L, y_Q, y_L) is a solution of the

Lagrangian problem. In particular, the coupling relation and complementary slackness conditions are satisfied.
ii) The values of the variables x_Q and y_Q are unique in optimal solutions of the primal and dual programs, respectively.

Proof: All requirements of the Lagrangian problem are satisfied automatically except the complementary slackness conditions and the relation $y_Q = P x_Q$. It remains to demonstrate that these conditions are satisfied. Let

$$\gamma = y_L^T (A_Q x_Q + A_L x_L - b)$$

$$\epsilon = x_Q^T (c_Q - A_Q^T y_L + y_Q) \tag{D-6}$$

$$\delta = x_L^T (c_L - A_L^T y_L)$$

represent the amount of dissatisfaction of the complementary slackness conditions. Under the constraints of the primal and dual problems, γ, ϵ, and δ must each be greater than or equal to zero. We have as the difference between the primal and dual objective functions

$$\phi(x_Q, x_L) - \theta(y_Q, y_L) =$$

$$= \frac{1}{2} x_Q^T P x_Q + c_Q^T x_Q + c_L^T x_L + \frac{1}{2} y_Q^T P^{-1} y_Q$$

$$- b^T y_L$$

Using the relations

$$b^T y_L = y_L A_Q x_Q + y_L^T A_L x_L - \gamma$$

$$c_Q^T x_Q = x_Q^T A_Q^T y_L - x_Q^T y_Q + \epsilon$$

$$c_L^T x_L = x_L^T A_L^T y_L + \delta$$

obtained from D-6 , we find

$$\phi(x_Q, x_L) - \theta(y_Q, y_L) = \frac{1}{2} [x_Q^T P x_Q - 2 x_Q^T y_Q +$$

$$+ y_Q^T P^{-1} y_Q] + \gamma + \epsilon + \delta$$

$$= \frac{1}{2} (x_Q - P^{-1} y_Q)^T (P x_Q - y_Q) + \gamma + \epsilon + \delta$$

$$= \frac{1}{2} (P x_Q - y_Q)^T P^{-1} (P x_Q - y_Q) + \gamma + \epsilon + \delta$$

Theorem D-2 shows that this quantity must be identically equal to zero. Each term of it is nonnegative; the first term because it is a positive definite form in the quantities $(P x_Q - y_Q)$, and the other terms as a result of the primal and dual constraints. Thus each term must vanish. This requires that the relation

$$y_Q = P x_Q$$

hold, and that the complementary slackness conditions be satisfied. Hence (x_Q, x_L, y_Q, y_L) is a solution of the Lagrangian problem.

To demonstrate the uniqueness property, let $(\overset{o}{x}_Q, \overset{o}{x}_L)$ and $(\overline{x}_Q, \overline{x}_L)$ be any two optimal solutions of the primal quadratic program. Theorem D-2 shows that the dual problem must possess an optimal solution (y_Q, y_L). According to the first assertion of the present theorem, we must have

$$y_Q = P \overset{o}{x}_Q$$

$$y_Q = P \overline{x}_Q$$

It follows that $\overset{o}{x}_Q = \overline{x}_Q$. In a similar manner the uniqueness of y_Q in optimal solutions of the dual may be shown.

Finally the selection of the particular formulation of the pair of dual quadratic program employed here will be justified. We shall show that the application of the duality principle to the dual problem yields the original primal problem.

The starting point is the dual problem,
    Maximize

$$\theta(\overline{y}_Q, \overline{y}_L) = -\frac{1}{2} \overline{y}_Q^T P^{-1} \overline{y}_Q + \overline{b}^T \overline{y}_L$$

subject to

$$\overline{A}_Q^T \overline{y}_L - \overline{y}_Q \leq \overline{c}_Q$$

$$\overline{A}_L^T \overline{y}_L \leq \overline{c}_L$$

$$\overline{y}_L \geq 0$$

146

in which we have barred the vectors and matrices to dis-
tinguish them in the following. By making the identifications

$$x_Q = \bar{y}_Q \qquad\qquad A_Q = \begin{bmatrix} I \\ 0 \end{bmatrix}$$

$$x_L = \bar{y}_L$$

$$c_Q = 0 \qquad\qquad A_L = \begin{bmatrix} -\bar{A}_Q^{\ T} \\ -\bar{A}_L^{\ T} \end{bmatrix}$$

$$c_L = -\bar{b} \qquad\qquad\qquad\qquad (D\text{-}7)$$

$$P = \bar{P}^{-1} \qquad\qquad b = \begin{bmatrix} -\bar{c}_Q \\ -\bar{c}_L \end{bmatrix}$$

we may express this problem in terms of a primal problem
in which x_Q is unrestricted:

Minimize

$$\frac{1}{2} x_Q^{\ T} P x_Q + c_Q^{\ T} x_Q + c_L^{\ T} x_L$$

subject to

$$A_Q x_Q + A_L x_L \geq b$$

$$x_L \geq 0$$

Therefore the dual for this problem has equalities for those
restrictions corresponding to the x_Q:

Maximize

$$-\frac{1}{2} y_Q P^{-1} y_Q + b^T y_L$$

subject to

$$A_Q^{\ T} y_L - y_Q = c_Q$$

$$A_L^{\ T} y_L \leq c_L$$

$$y_L \geq 0$$

Using the identifications D-7 we may write the dual of the dual problem:

Maximize

$$-\frac{1}{2} y_Q^{\ T} \bar{P} y_Q - \begin{bmatrix} \bar{c}_Q \\ \bar{c}_L \end{bmatrix} y_L$$

subject to

$$[I \quad 0] \ y_L - y_Q = 0 \qquad\qquad\qquad (D-8)$$

$$[-\bar{A}_Q - \bar{A}_L] \ y_L \leq -\bar{b}$$

If we identify y_L with

$$\begin{bmatrix} \bar{x}_Q \\ \bar{x}_L \end{bmatrix}$$

then D-8 requires that $y_Q = \bar{x}_Q$. We may rewrite the problem as

Minimize

$$\frac{1}{2} \bar{x}_Q \bar{P} \bar{x}_Q + \bar{c}_Q^{\ T} \bar{x}_Q + \bar{c}_L^{\ T} \bar{x}_L$$

subject to

$$\bar{A}_Q \bar{x}_Q + \bar{A}_L \bar{x}_L \geq \bar{b}$$

$$\bar{x}_Q \geq 0 \quad \bar{y}_Q \geq 0$$

which is precisely our primal problem as was to be shown.

Appendix E

Some Properties of Concave Functions

The objective in the three theorems of this section is to show that to any strictly concave function φ there is a corresponding strictly convex function θ such that

$$\partial \theta = - (\partial \phi)^{-1}$$

that is, the differential of the second is the negative inverse of the map which is the differential of the first.

The notation [x, y] will be used here to denote the dot product of the vectors x and y ; φ ∘ θ will denote the composition of the maps (functions) φ and θ. R^n is the Euclidian space of n dimensions. Page references in brackets are to several standard results in analysis in the treatise by Buck[*]. First we define the notions of concave and convex functions.

Definition: A mapping φ: D → R defined on a region D in R^n is concave if and only if for every x , y in D,

$$\phi [(1 - a) x + ay] \leq (1 - a) \phi(x) + a \phi (y) \qquad (E-1)$$

for all a , 0 < a < 1. Such a map is strictly concave if and only if E-1 holds as a strict inequality for all pairs of distinct points in D. It is convex (strictly convex) if and only if -φ is concave (strictly concave).

A generalization of the strictly increasing property [p. 20] of a function of a single variable will be used in this development.

Definition: Let t: D → R^n be a continuous transformation [p. 165] defined on a region D in R^n. We will say t has the strict increase property if and only if the following relation is satisfied for every pair of distinct points x and y in D:

$$[t(x), (y - x)] < [t(y), (y - x)]$$

The transformation t has the strict decrease property if and only if - t has the strict increase property.

The following two lemmas will be used in the proof of Theorem E-1. Since the proofs of the lemmas are fairly long although straightforward, and their assertions are reasonably obvious, these proofs will be omitted for the sake of brevity.

---

[*] R. C. Buck, Advanced Calculus, McGraw-Hill, 1956.

Lemma E-1: Let $[0, 1]$ be the closed unit interval in R. Let $\phi : I \to R$ be a function defined on some open interval I containing $[0, 1]$ and having a continuous derivative ϕ'. Suppose $\phi'(1) \leq \phi'(0)$. Then for some a, $0 < a < 1$,

$$\phi(a) \geq (1 - a) \phi(0) + a \phi(1)$$

Lemma E-2: Let $\phi : I \to R$ be a differentiable function defined on the unit interval $[0, 1]$. Suppose for some a, $0 < a < 1$,

$$\phi(a) \geq (1 - a) \phi(0) + a \phi(1)$$

Then there are two distinct points ξ and η, $0 < \xi < a < \eta < 1$, such that

$$\phi'(\xi) \geq \phi'(\eta)$$

Theorem E-1: Let D be a convex region in R^n, and let $\phi : D \to R$ be a function with continuous first derivatives. Let $t : D \to R^n$ be the differential [pp. 180-184] of ϕ. Then ϕ is strictly concave (convex) if and only if t has the strict increase (decrease) property.

Proof: We will demonstrate the theorem for the case in which ϕ is strictly concave. The other case follows from this by considering $-\phi$.

    1) ϕ strictly concave implies t has the strict increase property. Suppose t does not have the strict increase property. Then there exist distinct points x and y in D such that

$$[t(x), (y - x)] \geq [t(y), (y - x)]$$

Define the real-valued function $\eta(\xi)$ on some open interval containing $[0, 1]$ by

$$\eta(\xi) = f \circ \phi(\xi)$$

where

$$h(\xi) = x + (y - x)\xi$$

The derivative of $\eta(\xi)$ may be found by use of the chain rule [p. 191], as

$$\eta'(\xi) = [t \circ h(\xi), h'(\xi)]$$

$$= [t \circ h(\xi), (y - x)]$$

Thus

$$\eta'(0) = [t(x), (y - x)]$$

$$\eta'(1) = [t(y), (y - x)]$$

and it follows that $\eta'(0) \geq \eta'(1)$. From Lemma E-1 there is a point a in the open interval $(0, 1)$ such that

$$\eta(a) \geq (1 - a) \eta(0) + a \eta(1)$$

However, $h(0) = x$, $h(1) = y$, so that

$$\eta(0) = \phi(x), \ \eta(1) = \phi(y)$$

$$\eta(a) = \phi \circ h (a) = \phi[(1 - a) x + a y]$$

Thus

$$\theta[(1 - a) x + a y] \geq (1 - a) \phi(x) + a \phi(y)$$

in contradiction to the strict concavity of ϕ.

2) t having the strict increase property implies ϕ is concave. Suppose ϕ is not concave. Then there are distinct points x, y, in D, such that for some a, $0 < a < 1$:

$$\phi[(1 - a) x + ay] \geq (1 - a) \phi(x) + a \phi(y) \qquad \text{(E-2)}$$

Again define $\eta(\xi)$ as before by

$$\eta(\xi) = \phi \circ h (\xi)$$

where $h(\xi) = x + (y - x)\xi$ and, we may write in place of E-2

$$\eta(a) \geq (1 - a) \eta(0) + a \eta(1)$$

According to Lemma E-2 there exist ξ_1 and ξ_2, $0 < \xi_1 < a < \xi_2 < 1$, such that

$$\eta'(\xi_1) \geq \eta'(\xi_2)$$

However, we have as before

$$\eta'(\xi) = [t \circ h(\xi), (y - x)]$$

Thus

$$[t \circ h(\xi_1), (y - x)] \geq [t \circ h(\xi_2), (y - x)]$$

If we let $x_1 = h(\xi_1)$, $y_1 = h(\xi_2)$, and note that $(y_1 - x_1)$ has the same direction as $(y - x)$, we have

$$[\, t(x_1),\ (y_1 - x_1)\,] \geq [\, t(y_1),\ y_1 - x_1\,]$$

Thus t does not have the strict increase property, and the assertion is verified.

Theorem E-2: Let D be a region in R^n, and let $\phi: D \to R$ be a function with continuous first derivatives. Let t be the differential of ϕ . Then if ϕ is either strictly concave or strictly convex, $t: D \to R^n$ is a one-to-one map.

Proof: We give the proof for ϕ strictly concave. By Theorem E-1, t has the strict increase property. Suppose t is not one-to-one. Then there are distinct points x and y in D such that

$$t(x) = t(y)$$

It follows that

$$[t(x),\ (y - x)] = [t(y),\ (y - x)]$$

contradicting the assumption that t has the strict increase property.

Theorem E-3: Let D be a region in R^n, and let $t: D \to R^n$ be a continuous transformation having the strict increase property. Let E be a convex region in the range of t. Then t^{-1} exists and has the strict increase property on E.

Proof: Theorems E-1 and E-2 show that t is a one-to-one transformation. Hence t^{-1} exists. Suppose t^{-1} does not have the strict increase property. Then there are distinct points u and v in E such that

$$[t^{-1}(u),\ (v - u)] \geq [t^{-1}(v),\ (v - u)] \tag{E-3}$$

Let $x = t^{-1}(u)$, $y = t^{-1}(v)$, so that x and y are in D. Since t has the strict increase property,

$$[t(x),\ (y - x)] < [t(y),\ (y - x)]$$

or

$$[u,\ y] - [u,\ x] < [v,\ y] - [v,\ x]$$

From E-3 we have

$$[x, v] - [x, u] \geq [y, v] - [y, u]$$

which is a contradiction.

The preceding development has demonstrated the following facts: Any strictly concave function ϕ has a differential $\partial \phi$ which is one-to-one and has the strict increase property. The negative inverse of this map $(\partial \phi)^{-1}$ has the strict decrease property and is the differential of some convex function θ. That is, $\partial \theta = - (\partial \phi)^{-1}$.

For any strictly concave function ϕ, the function θ defined by the formula

$$\theta(y) = \phi \circ (\partial \phi)^{-1} (y) - [\, y, (\partial \phi)^{-1}(y)\,]$$

is called the <u>Legendre transformation</u> of ϕ. Its differential may be computed by the use of the chain rule [p. 191].

$$\partial \theta(y) = [\partial \phi \circ (\partial \phi)^{-1}(y),\, d(\partial \phi)^{-1}(y)] - [y,\, d(\partial \phi)^{-1}(y)] -$$

$$- (\partial \phi)^{-1}(y)$$

$$= [(\partial \phi) \circ (\partial \phi)^{-1}(y) - y\, ,\, d(\partial \phi)^{-1}(y)] - (\partial \phi)^{-1}(y)$$

$$= - (\partial \phi)^{-1}(y)$$

Thus the differential of θ is precisely the negative inverse of the differential of ϕ. Theorems E-1, E-2, and E-3 then show that, since ϕ is strictly concave, $\partial \phi$ has the strict increase property and, therefore, that $-(\partial \phi)^{-1}$ exists and has the strict decrease property. Thus θ is a strictly convex function.

Appendix F

Duality Relations in Concave Programming

Based on the properties of the Legendre transform developed in Appendix E, the duality principle will be extended to a class of concave and convex programming problems. Specifically, the discussion will concern a primal problem in which the objective function is a strictly concave function ϕ of variables x_C plus a linear combination of a distinct set of variables x_L,

Primal concave program

Find an (x_C, x_L) which

minimizes

$$\phi(x_C) + c^T x_L$$

with

$$A_L x_L + A_C x_C \geq b$$

$$x_L \geq 0, \quad x_C \geq 0$$

and a dual problem in which the Legendre transform of ϕ appears,

Dual convex program

Find the (y_C, y_L) which

maximizes

$$\theta(y_C) + b^T y_L$$

subject to

$$A_C^T y_L - y_C \leq 0$$

$$A_C^T y_L \geq c$$

$$y_C \text{ unrestricted}, \quad y_L \geq 0$$

Here the Legendre transform θ is defined by

$$\theta(y_C) = \phi \circ (\partial \phi)^{-1}(y_C) - [\ y_C, (\partial \phi)^{-1}(y_C)\ ] \qquad (F-1)$$

and has the property that

$$\partial \theta(y_C) = -(\partial \phi)^{-1}(y_C)$$

as was shown in Appendix E. In view of this property both the concave and the convex programming problem given above have the same corresponding Lagrangian problem.

Concave programming Lagrangian problem

Find (x_L, x_C, y_L, y_C) such that

$$A_C x_C + A_L x_L \geq b \qquad \qquad \text{primal} \atop \text{constraints} \qquad \text{(F-2)}$$

$$x_L \geq 0, \quad x_C \geq 0$$

$$A_C^T y_L - y_C \leq 0$$

$$A_L^T y_L \leq c \qquad \qquad \text{dual} \atop \text{constraints} \qquad \text{(F-3)}$$

$$y_L \geq 0$$

$$x_C = -\partial \theta(y_C) = (\partial \phi)^{-1}(y_C) \qquad \text{primal-dual} \atop \text{coupling} \qquad \text{(F-4)}$$

$$y_L^T(A_L x_L + A_C x_C - b) = 0$$

$$x_C^T(y_C - A_C^T y_L) \qquad = 0 \qquad \text{complementary} \atop {\text{slackness} \atop \text{conditions}} \qquad \text{(F-5)}$$

$$x_L^T(c - A_L^T y_L) \qquad = 0$$

Application of the fundamental theorem of non-linear programming to the dual pair of concave programs gives the following theorem which forms the basis for the proofs of this appendix.

Theorem F-1: A feasible vector (x_C, x_L) of the primal concave program is an optimal vector if and only if there is a (y_C, y_L) such that (x_C, x_L, y_C, y_L) is a solution of the concave programming Lagrangian problem. Likewise, a feasible vector of the dual convex program is optimal if and only if there is an (x_C, x_L) such that (x_C, x_L, y_C, y_L) solves the Lagrangian problem.

Two properties of the pair of concave programs will be demonstrated which are analogous to those proved for the dual pair of quadratic programs. First, however, a lemma is necessary.

155

Lemma F-1: If $\phi(x)$ is a strictly concave function and the strictly convex function $\theta(y)$ is its Legendre transform, then the quantity

$$\psi(x, y) = \phi(x) - \theta(y) - y^T x$$

is never negative and is zero if and only if

$$x = - \partial \theta(y) = (\partial \phi)^{-1}(y)$$

Proof: Employing the defining formula (F-1) for the Legendre transformation

$$\psi(x, y) = \phi(x) - \phi \circ (\partial \phi)^{-1}(y)$$

$$+ [y, (\partial \phi)^{-1}(y)] - y^T x$$

Let
$$w = (\partial \phi)^{-1}(y) \text{ so that } y = \partial\phi(w)$$

Then
$$\psi(x, y) = \phi(x) - \phi(w) - [\partial \phi(w), (x - w)]$$

If $x = (\partial \phi)^{-1}(y) = w$, then ψ is obviously zero. Now suppose x is distinct from w. According to the mean value theorem for a function of several variables [Buck,[*] p. 199] there is a point z on the line segment joining x and w such that

$$[\partial \phi(z), (x - w)] = \phi(x) - \phi(w) \qquad (F-6)$$

Also, since $\partial\phi$ has the strict increase property,

$$[\partial \phi(z), (z - w) > [\partial\phi(w), (z - w)]$$

or, since (z - w) is parallel to (x - w),

$$[\partial \phi(z), (x - w)] - [\partial \phi(w), (x - w)] > 0$$

Using F-6 this becomes

$$\phi(x) - \phi(w) - [\partial \phi(w), (x - w)] = \psi (x, y) > 0$$

Hence, $\psi(x, y)$ is strictly greater than zero except when $x = w = (\partial \phi)^{-1}(y)$.

---

[*] R. C. Buck, Advanced Calculus, McGraw-Hill, 1956.

Property F-1: If (x_C, x_L) and (y_C, y_L) are feasible solutions of the primal concave and the dual convex programs, respectively, then

$$\phi(x_C) + c^T x_C \geq \theta(y_C) + b^T y_L$$

Proof: By multiplying the constraints of the primal concave program by y_L, one obtains

$$y_L^T A_C x_C + y_L^T A_L x_L \geq b^T y_L$$

Similarly, from the constraints of the dual problem we have

$$x_C^T A_C^T y_L - x_C^T y_C \leq 0$$

$$x_L^T A_L^T y_L \leq c^T x_L$$

The difference between the objective functions of the primal and dual programs is

$$\Delta = \phi(x_C) + c^T x_L - \theta(y) - b^T y_L$$

or, using the above relations,

$$\Delta \geq \phi(x_C) - \theta(y_C) - y_C^T x_C$$

This quantity is never negative by Lemma F-1.

Property F-2: If (x_C, x_L) and (y_C, y_L) are feasible vectors for the primal and dual programs, and $\phi(x_C) + c^T x_L \leq \theta(y_C) + b^T y_L$, then (x_C, x_L) and $y_C, y_L)$ are optimal solutions of the primal and dual problems.

Proof: By Property F-1, $\phi(x_C) + c^T x_L \geq \theta(y_C) + b^T y_L$. Therefore the objective functions must be equal. If (x_C, x_L) is not optimal, then some other feasible vector must give a lower value of the primal objective function, and this would violate Property F-1. The same reasoning applies to (y_C, y_L) in relation to the dual problem.

The duality theorem and complementary slackness principle for concave programming may now be demonstrated.

Theorem F-2: (Duality Theorem) A feasible vector (x_C, x_L) for the primal concave program is optimal if and only if there is a feasible vector of the dual program such that the objective functions are equal.

$$\phi(x_C) + c^T x_L = \theta(y_C) + b^T y_L$$

A feasible vector of the dual is optimal if and only if there is a feasible vector of the primal such that the objectives are equal.

Proof: Only the first assertion will be demonstrated here as the proof of the second is essentially the same. In view of Property F-2 the sufficiency of the condition is clear. To show the necessity, suppose (x_C, x_L) is an optimal vector of the primal concave program. Then by Theorem F-1 there exists a (y_C, y_L) such that (x_C, x_L, y_C, y_L) is a solution of the concave programming Lagrangian problem. This (y_C, y_L) is then a feasible vector of the dual convex program. The difference between the primal and dual objective functions is

$$\Delta = \phi(x_C) + c^T x_L - \theta(y_C) - b^T y_L$$

Using the complementary slackness conditions F-5 , this becomes

$$\Delta = \phi(x_C) - y_C^T x_C - \theta(y_C)$$

The coupling relation and Lemma F-1 show that $\Delta = 0$.

Theorem F-3: (Complementary Slackness Principle and Uniqueness) i) If (x_C, x_L) is any optimal vector of the primal program and (y_C, y_L) is any optimal vector of the dual program, then (x_C, x_L, y_C, y_L) is a solution of the concave programming Lagrangian problem. In particular, the coupling relation and complementary slackness conditions are satisfied. ii) The values of the variables x_C and y_C are unique in the optimal vectors of the primal and dual programs, respectively.

Proof: All requirements of the Lagrangian problem are satisfied automatically except the complementary slackness conditions F-5 and the coupling relations $x_C = (\partial \phi)^{-1}(y_C)$. It remains to demonstrate that these conditions are satisfied. Let

158

$$\gamma = y_L^T(A_L x_L + A_C x_C - b)$$

$$\epsilon = x_L^T(y_C - A_C^T y_L)$$

$$\delta = x_L^T(c - A_L^T y_L)$$

represent the amount of dissatisfaction of the complementary slackness conditions. Under the constraints of the primal and dual problems γ, ϵ, and δ must each be greater than or equal to zero. The difference between the primal and dual objective functions is then

$$\phi(x_C) + c^T x_L - \theta(y_C) - b^T y_L$$

$$= [\phi(x_C) - \theta(y_C) - y_C^T x_C] + \gamma + \epsilon + \delta$$

(F-7)

Each term of the above expression is nonnegative: The first as a consequence of Lemma F-1 and the others by construction. Theorem F-2, however, requires that the primal and dual objective functions be equal and, hence, that the expression F-7 vanish. Since each term is nonnegative, they must vanish separately. In the case of the first term, Lemma F-1 shows that the coupling relation F-4 must be satisfied, and the other terms require that the complementary slackness conditions be met. Thus (x_C, x_L, y_C, y_L) is a solution of the Lagrangian problem.

To demonstrate the uniqueness property, let $(\overset{o}{x}_C, \overset{o}{x}_L)$ and $(\overline{x}_C, \overline{x}_L)$ be any two optimal vectors for the primal concave program. Theorem F-2 shows that the dual problem must possess an optimal vector (y_C, y_L). According to the first assertion of the present theorem, we must have both

$$\overset{o}{y}_C = \partial\phi(x_C)$$

$$\overline{y}_C = \partial\phi(x_C)$$

It follows that $\overset{o}{x}_C = \overline{x}_C$ because $\partial\phi$ is a one-to-one map. In a similar manner the uniqueness of y_C in optimal vectors of the dual program may be shown.

Appendix G

Properties of Terminal Pair Solutions

In this section the properties of the terminal pair system

η	x	ξ	y	v	
	A	e			b
	-Q		A^T	I	c
1			e^T		0

will be studied. In particular, the purpose of this development is to demonstrate that the set of all pairs (ξ, η) which correspond to solutions of the system is a breakpoint curve in the plane. Writing the system out, one has the three relations

$$A x + e \xi = b \qquad\qquad\qquad (G\text{-}1a)$$

$$A^T y - Q x + v = c \qquad\qquad\qquad (G\text{-}1b)$$

$$\eta = - e^T y \qquad\qquad\qquad (G\text{-}1c)$$

and the complementary slackness conditions,

$$x \geq 0, \quad v \geq 0, \quad x^T v = 0 \qquad\qquad\qquad (G\text{-}1d)$$

The matrices in G-1 are supposed to have the following properties:

    A - arbitrary rectangular matrix

    b, c, e - arbitrary column matrices

    Q - symmetric, positive semidefinite

First, a precise definition of what is meant by a breakpoint curve must be given.

Definition: A breakpoint curve is a sequence of k line segments in the plane with the following properties:
1) The first segment is a ray with non-zero direction vector (ξ, η) where $\xi \leq 0$, $\eta \leq 0$.
2) The kth segment (not necessarily distinct from the first) is a ray with non-zero direction vector (ξ, η) where $\xi \geq 0$, $\eta \geq 0$.

3) Let $(\overset{o}{\xi}_i,\ \overset{o}{\eta}_i)$ be the lower endpoint of the ith segment (except for the first), and let $(\overline{\xi}_i,\ \overline{\eta}_i)$ be the upper end point of the ith segment (except for the last). Then

$$\overset{o}{\xi}_{i+1} = \overline{\xi}_i,\quad \overset{o}{\eta}_{i+1} = \overline{\eta}_i,\quad i = 1,\ \ldots,\ k - 1$$

that is, succeeding segments must join in a common point.

4) Each segment must not have a negative slope.

$$\overline{\xi}_i - \overset{o}{\xi}_i \geq 0$$
$$\overline{\eta}_i - \overset{o}{\eta}_i \geq 0 \qquad,\quad i = 2,\ \ldots,\ k - 1$$

Definition: A terminal solution of a terminal-pair system is a pair (ξ, η) which corresponds to some solution of the system.

The following property of the terminal solutions will be frequently used in the proofs:

Lemma G-1: If $(\overline{\eta},\ \overline{x},\ \overline{\xi},\ \overline{y},\ \overline{v})$ and $(\eta,\ x,\ \xi,\ y,\ v)$ are any two solutions of the system, then

$$\xi\,\overline{\eta} = x^T c - \overline{y}^T b + x^T Q\,\overline{x} - \overline{v}^T x$$

Proof: By straight forward calculation, using relations G-1c , G-1a , and G-1b in succession, one finds

$$\xi\,\overline{\eta} = -\xi\,e^T\overline{y}$$
$$= y^T A x - y^T b$$
$$= x^T c - \overline{y}^T b + x^Y Q\,\overline{x} - \overline{v}^T x$$

First it will be shown that the set of terminal solutions of the system has a "monotone increase property"; namely, if ξ is increased η does not decrease, and vice versa.

Lemma G-2: Let $(\overset{o}{\xi}, \overset{o}{\eta})$ and $(\overline{\xi}, \overline{\eta})$ be terminal solutions of the system G-1 . Then

$$(\overline{\xi} - \overset{o}{\xi})\,(\overline{\eta} - \overset{o}{\eta}) \geq 0$$

Proof: Let $(\overline{\eta},\ \overline{x},\ \overline{\xi},\ \overline{y},\ \overline{v})$ and $(\overset{o}{\eta},\ \overset{o}{x},\ \overset{o}{\xi},\ \overset{o}{y},\ \overset{o}{v})$ be any solutions of G-1 corresponding to the given terminal solutions. Applying Lemma G-1, one obtains

$$(\bar{\xi} - \overset{o}{\xi})(\bar{\eta} - \overset{o}{\eta}) = \bar{\xi}\,\bar{\eta} + \overset{o}{\xi}\,\overset{o}{\eta} - \bar{\xi}\,\overset{o}{\eta} - \overset{o}{\xi}\,\bar{\eta}$$

$$= \bar{x}^T c + \overset{o}{x}{}^T c - \bar{x}^T c - \overset{o}{x}{}^T c$$

$$+ \bar{y}^T c + \overset{o}{y}{}^T c - \overset{o}{y}{}^T c - \bar{y}^T c$$

$$+ \bar{x}^T Q\, \bar{x} + \overset{o}{x}{}^T Q\, \overset{o}{x} - \bar{x}^T Q\, \overset{o}{x} - \overset{o}{x}{}^T Q\, \bar{x}$$

$$- \bar{v}^T \bar{x} - \overset{o}{v}{}^T \overset{o}{x} + \overset{o}{v}{}^T \bar{x} + \bar{v}^T \overset{o}{x}$$

$$= (\bar{x} - \overset{o}{x})^T Q(\bar{x} - \overset{o}{x}) + \bar{v}^T \overset{o}{x} + \overset{o}{v}{}^T \bar{x} \;\geq\; 0.$$

This expression is never less than zero because it is the sum of a positive definite form and products of nonnegative vectors.

Next the existence of line segments in the plane of which all points are terminal solutions will be shown. In any solution of G-1 , some components of x and some components of v must be zero in order that the complementary slackness condition be satisfied. Define a <u>primal</u> <u>variable</u> <u>set</u> P and a <u>dual</u> <u>variable</u> <u>set</u> D such that

$$i \text{ not in } P \text{ implies } x_i = 0$$

$$i \text{ not in } D \text{ implies } v_i = 0$$

A choice of the sets P and D is <u>allowable</u> if each i is contained in one and only one of P and D.

Lemma G-3: Let P and D be an allowable pair of primal and dual variable sets. Let S be the set of all terminal solutions (ξ, η) which correspond to solutions of the terminal-pair system consistent with P and D. Then either S is empty, S is a single point, or S is a line segment (possibly semi-infinite or infinite).

Proof: Let $(\bar{\xi}, \bar{\eta})$ and $(\overset{o}{\xi}, \overset{o}{\eta})$ be two distinct members of S, and let $(\bar{\eta}, \bar{x}, \bar{\xi}, \bar{y}, \bar{v})$ and $(\overset{o}{\eta}, \overset{o}{x}, \overset{o}{\xi}, \overset{o}{u}, \overset{o}{v})$ be corresponding solutions of G-1 consistent with P and D. Then, by direct substitution in G-1 :

$$
\begin{bmatrix} \eta \\ x \\ \xi \\ y \\ v \end{bmatrix} = (1 - a) \begin{bmatrix} \overline{\eta} \\ \overline{x} \\ \overline{\xi} \\ \overline{y} \\ \overline{v} \end{bmatrix} + a \begin{bmatrix} \overset{o}{\eta} \\ \overset{o}{x} \\ \overset{o}{\xi} \\ \overset{o}{y} \\ \overset{o}{v} \end{bmatrix}
$$

is also such a solution for $0 < a \leq 1$. Hence all points on the line segment joining $(\overline{\xi}, \overline{\eta})$ and $(\overset{o}{\xi}, \overset{o}{\eta})$ are terminal solutions and members of S.

Now let $(\overset{*}{\xi}, \overset{*}{\eta})$ be any member of S distinct from $(\overline{\xi}, \overline{\eta})$, and it will be shown that this point lies on the line determined by $(\overline{\xi}, \overline{\eta})$ and $(\overset{o}{\xi}, \overset{o}{\eta})$. Specifically, it will be shown that

$$
(\overset{*}{\xi} - \overline{\xi}) (\overset{o}{\eta} - \overline{\eta}) = (\overset{o}{\xi} - \overline{\xi}) (\overset{*}{\eta} - \overline{\eta})
$$

This is true only if the line joining $(\overline{\xi}, \overline{\eta})$ and $(\overset{*}{\xi}, \overset{*}{\eta})$ is parallel to, and hence identical with, the line joining $(\overline{\xi}, \overline{\eta})$ and $(\overset{o}{\xi}, \overset{o}{\eta})$. Using the same method as in Lemma G-2, one finds

$$
(\overset{*}{\xi} - \overline{\xi}) (\overset{o}{\eta} - \overline{\eta}) = (\overset{*}{x} - \overline{x})^T Q (\overset{o}{x} - \overline{x})
$$

and

$$
(\overset{o}{\xi} - \overline{\xi}) (\overset{*}{\eta} - \overline{\eta}) = (\overset{o}{x} - \overline{x})^T Q (\overset{*}{x} - \overline{x})
$$

Since the right hand sides are identical, the proof is complete.

The next property shows that there is a unique intersection between the set of terminal solutions and any 45° line of negative slope.

Lemma G-4: If the system G-1 has any solution then for every value of a scalar a there is a unique terminal solution (ξ, η) of the system which satisfies the condition

$$
\eta + \xi = a \tag{G-2}
$$

Proof: Consider the system of relations formed by appending the above condition to the terminal pair system:

$$A x + e \xi = b$$

$$x \geq 0$$

$$A^T y - Q x + v = c \qquad \text{(G-3)}$$

$$\eta = -e^T y$$

$$\xi + \eta = a$$

$$v \geq 0$$

$$v^T x = 0$$

These relations comprise the Lagrangian problem associated with the following quadratic programming problem.
Minimize

$$\frac{1}{2} x^T Q x + c^T x + \frac{1}{2} \xi^2 - a \xi \qquad \text{(G-4a)}$$

with

$$A x + e \xi = b \qquad \text{(G-4b)}$$

$$x \geq 0$$

By assumption the terminal pair system has some solution (η, x, ξ, y, v). If we take $a = \xi - e^T y$, then (η, x, ξ, y, v) is a solution of the Lagrangian problem G-3 for this value of a. Hence (x, ξ) is an optimal solution of the quadratic program G-4. It will be shown that the objective function G-4a is bounded below on any ray in the constraint set G-4b, regardless of the value of a. This implies that G-4 has an optimal vector for each a and, hence, that G-3 has a solution for every a.

A ray in the constraint set G-4b is described by

$$x = \overset{o}{x} + \lambda$$
$$\xi = \overset{o}{\xi} + \lambda \qquad , \lambda \geq 0$$

where

$$A \overset{o}{x} + e \overset{o}{\xi} \geq b$$

$$\overset{o}{x} \geq 0$$

$$A \overline{x} + e \overline{\xi} \geq 0$$

$$\overline{x} \geq 0$$

The objective function G-4a evaluated on this ray is

$$\phi(\lambda) = \frac{1}{2}(\overset{o}{x} + \lambda\,\overline{x})^T Q\,(\overset{o}{x} + \lambda\,\overline{x}) + c^T(\overset{o}{x} + \lambda\,\overline{x}) +$$

$$+ \frac{1}{2}(\overset{o}{\xi} + \lambda\,\overline{\xi})^2 - a(\overset{o}{\xi} + \lambda\,\overline{\xi})$$

$$= \phi(0) + \frac{1}{2}\lambda^2(\overline{x}^T Q\,\overline{x} + \overline{\xi}^2) + \lambda\,(\overset{oT}{x} Q\,\overline{x} + c^T\overline{x} + \overset{o}{\xi}\,\overline{\xi} - a\,\overline{\xi})$$

This is certainly bounded below if the coefficient of λ^2 is strictly positive. On the other hand, for a ray in which the coefficient of λ^2 is zero (which requires $\overline{\xi} = 0$), the objective function is

$$\phi(\lambda) = \lambda\,(\overset{oT}{x} Q\,\overline{x} + c^T\,\overline{x})$$

Since this is bounded below for some a, it must be bounded below for all a. This establishes the existence of a solution to G-3 for every a. It remains to show that the corresponding terminal solution is unique.

Suppose there are two terminal solutions, $(\overset{o}{\xi}, \overset{o}{\eta})$ and $(\overline{\xi}, \overline{\eta})$, which satisfy G-3 for the same value of a. Condition G-2 and Lemma G-1 yield

$$\overline{\xi}\,\overset{o}{\xi} = -\overline{\eta}\,\overset{o}{\xi} + a\overset{o}{\xi} = -c^T\overset{o}{x} + b^T\overline{y} - \overset{oT}{x}Q\,\overline{x} + \overline{v}^T\overset{o}{x} + a\overset{o}{\xi}$$

Now consider the product

$$\frac{1}{2}(\overline{\xi} - \overset{o}{\xi})^2 = -\frac{1}{2}\overline{\xi}^2 + \frac{1}{2}\overset{o}{\xi}^2 - \overline{\xi}\,\overset{o}{\xi} + \overline{\xi}^2$$

By applying the above result to the last two terms of this expression we obtain

$$\frac{1}{2}(\overline{\xi} - \overset{o}{\xi})^2 = \phi(\overset{o}{x}, \overset{o}{\xi}) - \phi(\overline{x}, \overline{\xi}) - \frac{1}{2}(\overline{x} - \overset{o}{x})^T Q(\overline{x} - \overset{o}{x}) - \overline{v}^T\overset{o}{x} \tag{G-6}$$

Since $(\overset{o}{x}, \overset{o}{\xi})$ and $(\overline{x}, \overline{\xi})$ must both be optimal solutions of G-4, they yield identical values of the objective function. The other terms on the right side of G-6 can never be greater than zero. The left side is never less than zero. Hence $\overline{\xi} = \overset{o}{\xi}$, and G-2 shows that $\overline{\eta} = \overset{o}{\eta}$.

The above result allows us to show that there is a ray of terminal solutions extending infinitely toward positive coordinate values and also a ray extending toward negative coordinate values.

Lemma G-5: For some allowable P and D the corresponding set of terminal solutions is a ray

$$(\xi, \eta) = (\overline{\xi}, \overline{\eta}) + \lambda \; (\overset{*}{\xi}, \overset{*}{\eta}), \quad \lambda \geq 0$$

where $\overset{*}{\xi} \leq 0$, $\overset{*}{\eta} \leq 0$ but at least one of $\overset{*}{\xi}$ and $\overset{*}{\eta}$ is non-zero. Also for some allowable P and D, the corresponding set of terminal solutions is a ray with $\overset{*}{\xi} \geq 0$, $\overset{*}{\eta} \geq 0$ where at least one of $\overset{*}{\xi}$ and $\overset{*}{\eta}$ is non-zero.

Proof: If all segments were finite, one could choose α sufficiently negative so that

$$\alpha < \overset{o}{\xi}_i + \overset{o}{\eta}_i \;, \text{ all } i$$

and there could be no terminal solution satisfying G-2 . The direction of the ray must be within the range specified so that Lemma G-2 is satisfied. Taking α to be sufficiently positive demonstrates the second assertion.

In the remaining proofs the term line segment refers to the non-empty set of terminal solutions of $\overline{G-1}$ for some allowable choice of P and D. A line segment may consist of only one point. Suppose there are k choices of the sets P and D for which there are associated line segments. The lower and upper end points of the ith line segment will be denoted by $(\overset{o}{\xi}_i, \overset{o}{\eta}_i)$ and $(\overline{\xi}_i, \overline{\eta}_i)$, respectively, where

$$\overset{o}{\xi}_i + \overset{o}{\eta}_i \; \leq \; \overline{\xi}_i + \overline{\eta}_i$$

Lemma G-6: The line segments comprising the set of terminal solutions can be arranged in a sequence L_1, L_2, ..., L_k so that

$$\overset{o}{\xi}_{i+1} + \overset{o}{\eta}_{i+1} \geq \overline{\xi}_i + \overline{\eta}_i, \quad i = 1, \ldots, k-1.$$

Proof: Take L_1 to be a line segment extending indefinitely toward negative η and/or ξ. Given L_1 through L_i, take L_{i+1} to be that one of the remaining segments for which $\overset{o}{\xi} + \overset{o}{\eta}$ is the smallest. Then

$$\overset{o}{\xi}_{i+1} + \overset{o}{\eta}_{i+1} \geq \overline{\xi}_i + \overline{\eta}_i \tag{G-7}$$

because

$$\overset{o}{\xi}_i + \overset{o}{\eta}_i \; \leq \; \overset{o}{\xi}_{i+1} + \overset{o}{\eta}_{i+1}$$

and if G-7 were not true, there would be a point on L_i with

$$\xi + \eta = \overset{o}{\xi}_{i+1} + \overset{o}{\eta}_{i+1}$$

This would contradict Lemma G-4 for $a = \overset{o}{\xi}_{i+1} + \overset{o}{\eta}_{i+1}$. The last segment L_k of the sequence is the segment extending indefinitely toward positive ξ and/or η.

<u>Theorem G-1</u>: The set of all terminal solutions of a terminal pair system is a breakpoint curve.

<u>Proof</u>: The preceding lemmas have shown that the set of all terminal solutions is a sequence of straight line segments with nonnegative slopes. It remains to demonstrate that these segments join to form a continuous curve, that is,

$$\begin{aligned}\overline{\xi}_i &= \overset{o}{\xi}_{i+1}\\ \overline{\eta}_i &= \overset{o}{\eta}_{i-1}\end{aligned} \quad,\quad i = 1, \ldots, k-1 \tag{G-8}$$

Suppose this were not true. Then for some i, G-8 is not satisfied. Lemma G-6 shows that

$$\overline{\xi}_i + \overline{\eta}_i \le \overset{o}{\xi}_{i+1} + \overset{o}{\eta}_{i+1} \tag{G-9}$$

If G-9 is satisfied as an equality both $(\overline{\xi}_i, \overline{\eta}_i)$ and $(\overset{o}{\xi}_{i+1}, \overset{o}{\eta}_{i+1})$ would be distinct solutions of the terminal pair system with

$$\overline{\xi}_i + \overline{\eta}_i = a = \overset{o}{\xi}_{i+1} + \overset{o}{\eta}_{i-1} \tag{G-10}$$

in violation of Lemma G-4. If G-9 is satisfied as an inequality there is no terminal solution satisfying G-10 with

$$a = \frac{1}{2}(\overline{\xi}_i + \overline{\eta}_i + \overset{o}{\xi}_{i+1} + \overset{o}{\eta}_{i+1})$$

again in violation of Lemma G-4.

To conclude this section two special classes of terminal pair systems are considered. In the first, the matrix Q is taken to be null, and it is shown that the corresponding breakpoint curve contains only horizontal and vertical segments. Secondly, Q and either b or c are taken to be zero. In the first instance all vertical segments collapse into the η-axis, and in the second, all horizontal segments collapse into the ξ-axis.

Theorem G-2:   The breakpoint curve for a terminal-pair
system consists only of vertical and horizontal line segments
when Q is the null matrix.

Proof: Let $(\overset{o}{\xi}, \overset{o}{\eta})$ and $(\overline{\xi}, \overline{\xi})$ be any two terminal solutions of
G-1 for the same segment (having the same primal and dual
active variable sets, P and D).   Lemma G-1 with Q set to
zero yields

$$(\overline{\xi} - \overset{o}{\xi})(\overline{\eta} - \overset{o}{\eta}) = (\overline{v} - \overset{o}{v})^T (\overline{x} - \overset{o}{x})$$

which is zero by the complementary slackness condition.
Hence either

$$(\overline{\xi} - \overset{o}{\xi}) > 0$$

or

$$(\overline{\eta} - \overset{o}{\eta}) > 0$$

but not both.   In the first case the segment must be horizontal; in
the second, vertical.

Theorem G-3: The breakpoint curve for a terminal-pair system
in which matrices Q and b are null contains no vertical segment in which ξ is not zero; if Q and c are null, it contains
no horizontal segment in which η is not zero.

Proof: Let $(\xi, \overset{o}{\eta})$ and $(\xi, \overline{\eta})$ be two terminal solutions of G-1
for the same vertical segment $(\overline{\eta} > \overset{o}{\eta})$.   Then, using Lemma
G-1 with Q and c set to zero, one has

$$\xi(\overline{\eta} - \overset{o}{\eta}) = \overline{v}^T x - \overset{o}{y}^T b + \overline{y}^T b + \overline{y}^T b = 0$$

hence $\xi = 0$ as required.   The second assertion is proved in
the same manner.

The following result concerning basic solutions of the terminal-
pair system is used in Chapter 5.

Lemma G-7:   Let $\overline{z}$ be a basic solution of the terminal-pair
system in which the conjugate variable pair (x_b, v_b) is at
breakpoint.   Let $\overset{o}{z}$ and $\overset{*}{z}$ be the unit incremental solutions
associated with this basic solution, and suppose $\overset{o}{x}_b > 0$, and $\overset{*}{v}_b > 0$,
$\overset{o}{v}_b = \overset{*}{x}_b = 0$.   Then

$$\overset{o}{\xi} \overset{*}{\eta} < \overset{*}{\xi} \overset{o}{\eta}$$

Proof: The incremental solutions $\overset{o}{z}$ and $\overset{*}{z}$ satisfy the terminal pair system with zero right hand side. Using Lemma G-1, we have

$$\overset{o}{\xi}\,\overset{*}{\eta} - \overset{*}{\xi}\,\overset{o}{\eta} = \overset{oT}{x}\,Q\,\overset{*}{x} - \overset{*T}{v}\,\overset{o}{x}$$

$$- \overset{*T}{x}\,Q\,\overset{o}{x} + \overset{oT}{v}\,\overset{*}{x}$$

$$= -\overset{*}{v}_b\,\overset{*}{x}_b < 0$$

Appendix H

The Generalized Breakpoint Stepping Method [*]

The algorithm developed in Chapter 5 for tracing the break-point curve of the terminal-pair system

η	x	ξ	y	v	
	A	e			b
	-Q		A^T	I	c
1			e^T		0

$$(\text{H-1})$$

fails if more than one conjugate variable pair is at breakpoint at some basic solution during the computation. In this appendix theoretical developments will be made which show how to modify the method so that it will work without exception. In order to resolve the degeneracy problem the original system of relations H-1 describing the breakpoint curve will be expanded so that, in a sense, breakpoints that were superimposed in the terminal-pair system become distinct in a generalized system. Each variable z_i of the original system is replaced by a vector Z_i of $m + n + 2$ components in the generalized system. The first component of the vector is identified with the original variable. Similarly each element d_i of the right hand side is replaced by a vector D_i. Hence the original system is replaced by

$$P \, Z^T = D^T \qquad (\text{H-2})$$

where

$$P = \begin{bmatrix} 0 & A & e & 0 & 0 \\ 0 & -Q & 0 & A^T & I \\ 1 & 0 & 0 & e^T & 0 \end{bmatrix}, \quad D = \begin{bmatrix} b^T & c^T & 0 \\ I & 0 & 0 \\ 0 & I & 0 \\ 0 & 0 & 1 \end{bmatrix}$$

and

$$Z = [\, g \quad X \quad f \quad Y \quad V \,]$$

Using this generalized system, it will be shown that the quantity $f + g$ increases strictly on each step of the breakpoint stepping algorithm. However, this increase is not in the ordinary algebraic sense, but in a special sense which is defined below.

---

[*]The methods employed in this appendix are due in part to Wolfe [11].

Definition: A vector x is <u>greater than zero</u> in the <u>lexicographic sense</u>, and one writes

$$x \overset{*}{\geq} 0$$

if x is not zero and its first nonzero component is positive. The vector is <u>less than zero</u>, and one writes

$$x \overset{*}{\leq} 0$$

if its negative is greater than zero. The relation

$$x \overset{*}{>} y$$

is true if

$$x - y \overset{*}{>} 0$$

Definition: A square matrix which is the product of two vectors

$$A = x\, y^T$$

is said to be greater than zero in the <u>lexicographic sense</u>, and one writes

$$A \overset{*}{>} 0$$

if A is not identically zero and

$$a_{ij} > 0$$

where i is the first nonzero row and j is the first nonzero column of A.

The following property is an immediate consequence of the definitions.

<u>Property H-1</u>: The relation $x\, y^T \overset{*}{\geq} 0$ is true if and only if

$$x \overset{*}{>} 0,\; y \overset{*}{>} 0 \quad \text{or} \quad x \overset{*}{<} 0,\; y \overset{*}{<} 0$$

The requirement that the variables x_i and v_i be nonnegative in the original system is replaced by the requirements

$$X_i \overset{*}{\geq} 0, \quad V_i \overset{*}{\geq} 0$$

in the generalized system. The complementary slackness condition

$$x_i \, v_i = 0 \, , \quad \text{all} \quad i$$

becomes

$$X_{ji} \, V_{ji} = 0 \, , \quad \text{all} \quad i \text{ and } j$$

that is, each component of the new vector variable must satisfy the same condition as the single variable in the original system.

It is clear that for any matrix Z which is a solution of the generalized system, the first components of the columns of Z form a solution of the original terminal-pair system.

Next, the notion of a basis will be defined for the generalized system.

Definition: A basic solution of the generalized system is a solution Z in which $n + 1$ of the columns of X and V are identically zero. The $m + n + 1$ columns of P corresponding to columns of Z not required to be zero comprise the basis associated with the basic solution. A basis must always include the columns of P corresponding to the vectors f, g, and the columns of Y.

The following property of a basis of the generalized system is crucial in succeeding arguments.

Lemma H-1: Let P_i, i in B be the basis vectors corresponding to some basic solution Z. Then these vectors form a linearly independent set and

$$Z_i \overset{*}{>} 0, \quad i \in B$$

Proof: The vectors of the basis P_i, $i \in B$ form an $m + n + 1$ by $m + n + 1$ square matrix R. The corresponding columns of Z form an $m + n + 2$ by $m + n + 1$ matrix W such that

$$R \, W^T = D^T = \begin{bmatrix} b & I & 0 & 0 \\ c & 0 & I & 0 \\ 0 & 0 & 0 & 1 \end{bmatrix}$$

The matrix D was constructed to have rank $m + n + 1$. Hence, both R and W must have rank $m + n + 1$. With respect to R, this shows that its columns are linearly independent; with respect to W this shows that none of its columns can be identically zero.

Thus each vector variable associated with a vector of the basis for any basic solution cannot be identically zero. On the other hand,

172

the complementary slackness condition requires that one member
of each pair of conjugate variables must be identically zero for
each solution. Since $n + 1$ of the X_i and V_i must be zero for a
basic solution, precisely one pair of conjugate variables must
have $X_i = 0$ and $V_i = 0$. The remaining X_i and V_i correspond
to vectors in the basis and therefore cannot be zero by the above
lemma.

Definition: For a basic solution the pair of conjugate variables
(X_b, V_b) for which $X_b = 0$ and $V_b = 0$ will be said to be at
breakpoint.

Since the vectors of the basis are linearly independent and form a
square matrix, the inverse of this matrix exists. The row of the
inverse corresponding to a column P_i in the basis will be represented by the column vector S_i. Hence

$$P_i^T S_j = \begin{cases} 1, & i = j \\ 0, & i \neq j \end{cases}, \quad i, j \in B$$

because the product of a matrix with its inverse is the identity
matrix.

The three theorems which follow show that, given a basic solution of the generalized system, either a new basic solution may be
formed with increased $f + g$ or a class of solutions is available
on which the quantity $f + g$ increases indefinitely. In Theorems
H-1 and H-2 the existence of a class of solutions for which $f + g$
increases and one for which $f + g$ decreases is demonstrated as
a preliminary for Theorem H-3 where the main result is proved.

Theorem H-1: Let $\overline{Z}$ be a basic solution of the generalized
system in which the conjugate variable pair (X_b, V_b) is at
breakpoint. Then a class of solutions $Z(h)$ can be constructed
for which $X_b(h) \overset{*}{>} 0$ for $h \overset{*}{>} 0$, and a class $Z(k)$ for which
$V_b(k) \overset{*}{>} 0$ for $k \overset{*}{>} 0$.

Proof: Let P_i, $i \in B$ be the basis associated with $\overline{Z}$, and
S_i, $i \in B$ be the vectors of the basis inverse. Suppose that
P_r is the column of P associated with the variable vector
X_b. P_r is not a member of the basis, but can be expressed
in terms of the linearly independent basis vectors.

$$P_r = I P_r = \sum_{i \in B} (P_i S_i^T) P_r$$

$$= \sum_{i \in B} (S_i^T P_r) P_i$$

Since $\overline{Z}$ is a basic solution

$$\sum_{i \in B} P_i \overline{Z}_i^{\,T} = D^T$$

Then

$$\sum_{i \in B} P_i \overline{Z}_i^{\,T} - P_r h^T + P_r h^T = D^T$$

or

$$\sum_{i \in B} P_i [\overline{Z}_i - (S_i^{\,T} P_r) h]^T + P_r h^T = D^T$$

Therefore

$$Z_i(h) = \begin{cases} \overline{Z}_i - (S_i^{\,T} P_r) h & i \in B \\ h & i = r \\ 0 & \text{other } i \end{cases}$$

is a solution of the generalized system for $h \overset{*}{\geq} 0$ as long as $(S_i^{\,T} P_r) h \overset{*}{\leq} \overline{Z}_i$ for all i in B corresponding to vector variables in X or V.

In a similar manner let P_s be the column of P associated with the variable vector V_b. P_s is not in the basis, but as above

$$P_s = \sum_{i \in B} (S_i^{\,T} P_s) P_i$$

and

$$Z_i(k) = \begin{cases} Z_i - (S_i^{\,T} P_s) k & i \in B \\ k & i = s \\ 0 & \text{other } i \end{cases}$$

is a solution of the modified system for $k \overset{*}{\geq} 0$ as long as

$$(S_i^{\,T} P_s) k \overset{*}{\leq} \overline{Z}_i$$

The proof of the next theorem requires two preliminary results.

$\underline{\text{Lemma H-2:}}$ Let $\overline{Z}$ be a basic solution of the generalized terminal-pair system in which the pair of conjugate variable vectors (X_b, V_b) is at breakpoint. Let

$$\overset{o}{Z} = Z(h), \qquad h \overset{*}{\geq} 0$$

and

$$\overset{*}{Z} = Z(k), \qquad k \overset{*}{>} 0$$

be the two classes of solutions formed in Theorem H-1. Then

$$(\overset{*}{f} - \overline{f})(\overset{*}{g} - \overline{g})^T \overset{*}{\geq} 0$$

and

$$(\overset{o}{f} - \overline{f})(\overset{o}{g} - \overline{g})^T \overset{*}{\geq} 0$$

$\underline{\text{Proof:}}$ It is clear that the difference between any two solutions of the generalized system is a solution of the system with its right hand side replaced by zero.

$$A(\overset{*}{X} - \overline{X})^T + e(\overset{*}{f} - \overline{f})^T = 0$$
$$- Q(\overset{*}{X} - \overline{X})^T + A^T(\overset{*}{Y} - \overline{Y})^T + (\overset{*}{V} - \overline{V})^T = 0$$
$$(\overset{*}{g} - \overline{g})^T + e^T(\overset{*}{Y} - \overline{Y})^T = 0$$

Multiplying these relations on the left by $(\overset{*}{Y} - \overline{Y})$, $(\overset{*}{X} - \overline{X})$ and $(\overset{*}{f} - \overline{f})$, respectively and combining yields

$$T = (\overset{*}{f} - \overline{f})(\overset{*}{g} - \overline{g})^T = (\overset{*}{X} - \overline{X})Q(\overset{*}{X} - \overline{X})^T + \overline{X}\overset{*}{V}^T + \overset{*}{X}\overline{V}^T$$

The (i, j) element of the square matrix T is

$$T_{ij} = [(\overset{*}{X}-\overline{X})^T]_i^T Q [(\overset{*}{X}-\overline{X})^T]_j + (\overline{X}^T)_i^T(\overset{*}{V}^T)_j + (\overset{*}{X}^T)_i^T(\overline{V}^T)_j$$

The complementary slackness condition shows that the last two terms are zero. (The only variable vector which was zero in $\overline{Z}$ but nonzero in $\overset{*}{Z}$ is $\overset{*}{V}_b$. However $\overset{o}{X}_b(h)$ is zero.) Then the matrix T is symmetric because Q is symmetric. Let r be the index of the first nonzero row of T (assuming T is not null). Then r is also the index of the first nonzero column and $T_{rr} \neq 0$. We have

$$T_{rr} = [\,(\overset{*}{X} - \overline{X})^T\,]^T_r\, Q\, [(\overset{*}{X} - \overline{X})^T]_r \geq 0$$

because Q is positive semidefinite. Thus $T_{rr} > 0$ and since T is the product of two vectors, it follows from Property H-1

$$T = (\overset{*}{f} - \overline{f})\,(\overset{*}{g} - \overline{g})^T \overset{*}{\geq} 0$$

The same argument proves the second assertion.

<u>Lemma H-3</u>: Let $\overline{Z}$ be a basic solution of the generalized terminal-pair system and let

$$\overset{o}{Z} = Z(h)\,, \qquad h \overset{*}{>} 0$$

and

$$\overset{*}{Z} = Z(k)\,, \qquad k \overset{*}{>} 0$$

be the two classes of solutions formed in Theorem H-1. Then

$$(\overset{*}{f} - \overline{f})\,(\overset{o}{g} - \overline{g})^T \overset{*}{>} (\overset{*}{g} - \overline{g})\,(\overset{o}{f} - \overline{f})^T$$

<u>Proof</u>: Let b be the index of the conjugate variable pair which is at breakpoint for the basic solution $\overline{Z}$. Then $\overset{o}{V_b} = 0$ and $\overset{*}{X_b} = 0$ while $\overset{o}{X_b} = h \overset{*}{>} 0$ and $\overset{*}{V_b} = k \overset{*}{>} 0$.

By manipulation similar to that used in the proof of Lemma H-2, one finds

$$(\overset{*}{f} - \overline{f})\,(\overset{o}{g} - \overline{g})^T - (\overset{*}{g} - \overline{g})\,(\overset{o}{f} - \overline{f})^T$$

$$= (\overset{*}{X} - \overline{X})\, Q\, (\overset{o}{X} - \overline{X})^T$$

$$- \overset{*}{X}\overset{o}{V}^T + \overset{*}{X}\overline{V}^T + \overline{X}\overset{o}{V}^T - \overline{X}\overline{V}^T$$

$$- (\overset{*}{X} - \overline{X})\, Q\, (\overset{o}{X} - \overline{X})^T$$

$$+ \overset{*}{V}\overset{o}{X}^T - \overline{V}\overset{o}{X}^T - \overset{*}{V}\overline{X}^T + \overline{V}\overline{X}^T$$

$$= - \overset{*}{X}\overset{o}{V}^T + \overset{*}{X}\overline{V}^T + \overline{X}\overset{o}{V}^T + \overset{*}{V}\overset{o}{X}^T - \overline{V}\overset{o}{X}^T - \overset{*}{V}\overline{X}^T$$

Now

$$\overline{X}\,\overset{o}{V}^T = 0$$

$$\overline{V}\overset{o}{X}{}^T = 0$$

because the same columns are nonzero in $\overset{o}{V}$ as in $\overline{V}$, and the only new nonzero column in $\overset{o}{X}$ is $\overset{o}{X}_b$, but it was postulated that $\overset{o}{V}_b = 0$. In the same manner

$$\overset{*}{V}\,\overline{X}^T = 0$$

$$\overset{*}{X}\,\overline{V}^T = 0$$

and

$$\overset{*}{X}\,\overset{o}{V}^T = 0$$

On the other hand

$$\overset{*}{V}\,\overset{o}{X}^T = \overset{*}{V}_b\overset{o}{X}_b^{\ T} = k\,h^T$$

Thus

$$(\overset{*}{f} - \overline{f})\,(\overset{o}{g} - \overline{g})^T - (\overset{*}{g} - \overline{g})(\overset{o}{f} - \overline{f})^T = k\,h^T \gtrless 0$$

verifying the assertion of the lemma.

Theorem H-2: Given a basic solution $\overline{Z}$ of the generalized system, and the two classes of solutions $\overset{o}{Z}(h)$ and $\overset{*}{Z}(k)$ constructed in Theorem H-1, one of these classes has

$$\overset{o}{f}(h) + \overset{o}{g}(h) \lessgtr \overline{f} + \overline{g}, \qquad h \gtrless 0$$

and the other has

$$\overset{*}{f}(k) + \overset{*}{g}(k) \gtrless \overline{f} + \overline{g}, \quad k \gtrless 0$$

Proof: From the proof of Theorem H-1, one has

$$\overset{o}{f}(h) = \overline{f} + \overset{o}{a}\,h \qquad\qquad \overset{o}{a} = S_f^T\,P_r$$

$$\overset{o}{g}(h) = \overline{g} + \overset{o}{\beta}h \qquad\qquad \overset{o}{\beta} = S_g^T\,P_r$$

$$\overset{*}{f}(k) = \overline{f} + \overset{*}{a}k \qquad\qquad \overset{*}{a} = S_f^T\,P_s$$

$$\overset{*}{g}(k) = \overline{g} + \overset{*}{\beta}k \qquad\qquad \overset{*}{\beta} = S_g^T\,P_s$$

In terms of this notation, Lemma H-2 states that

$$\overset{o}{a}\,h\,\overset{o}{\beta}\,h^T \gtrless 0 \qquad \text{which requires} \quad \overset{o}{a}\overset{o}{\beta} \geq 0 \qquad \text{(H-3)}$$

and

$$\overset{*}{a}\,k\,\overset{*}{\beta}k^T \gtrless 0 \qquad \text{which requires} \quad \overset{*}{a}\overset{*}{\beta} \geq 0 \qquad \text{(H-4)}$$

Also Lemma H-3 states that

$$\overset{*}{a}\, k\, \overset{o}{\beta}\, h^T \;>\; \overset{*}{\beta}\, k\, \overset{*}{a}\, h^T$$

which requires

$$\overset{*}{a}\, \overset{o}{\beta} \;>\; \overset{*}{\beta}\, \overset{o}{a} \qquad\qquad\qquad\qquad \text{(H-5)}$$

According to this relation $\overset{o}{a}$ and $\overset{o}{\beta}$ cannot both be zero, nor can both $\overset{*}{a}$ and $\overset{*}{\beta}$. It follows that the quantity $f + g$ must either increase or decrease for each of the two classes of general system solutions: it cannot remain fixed.

We shall assume that

$$\overset{o}{f} + \overset{o}{g} \;\gtrless\; \overline{f} + \overline{g} \qquad \text{for } h \overset{*}{\gtrless} 0 \qquad\qquad \text{(H-6)}$$

and show that

$$\overset{*}{f} + \overset{*}{g} \;\lessgtr\; \overline{f} + \overline{g} \qquad \text{for } k \overset{*}{\gtrless} 0 \qquad\qquad \text{(H-7)}$$

Relation H-6 requires $\overset{o}{a} + \overset{o}{\beta} > 0$. Suppose $\overset{*}{a} + \overset{*}{\beta} > 0$ and we will obtain a contradiction. Consider the product

$$T \;=\; (\overset{*}{f} - \overset{o}{f})\, (\overset{*}{g} - \overset{o}{g})^T$$

which must be $\overset{>}{\scriptstyle =} 0$ by Lemma H-2. Substitution yields

$$T \;=\; (\overset{*}{a} k - \overset{o}{a} h)\, (\overset{*}{\beta} k - \overset{o}{\beta} h)^T$$

Take some sufficiently small $h \overset{*}{>} 0$ and choose $k \overset{*}{>} 0$ such that

$$\frac{1}{\overset{o}{a} + \overset{o}{\beta}}\; k \;=\; \frac{1}{\overset{*}{a} + \overset{*}{\beta}}\; h \;=\; t \overset{*}{>} 0$$

Then

$$T \;=\; (\overset{*}{a}\,\overset{o}{\beta} - \overset{o}{a}\,\overset{*}{\beta})\, (\overset{*}{\beta}\,\overset{o}{a} - \overset{o}{\beta}\,\overset{*}{a})\, t\, t^T$$

and relation H-5 shows that $T \overset{<}{\scriptstyle =} 0$ in violation of Lemma H-2.

It follows that to satisfy H-4 and H-5 we must have $\overset{*}{a} + \overset{*}{\beta} < 0$ and H-7 is an immediate consequence. Similarly, assuming

$$\overset{o}{f} + \overset{o}{g} \;\lessgtr\; \overline{f} + \overline{g} \qquad \text{for } h \overset{*}{\gtrless} 0$$

leads to the conclusion that

$$\overset{*}{f} + \overset{*}{g} \;\overset{*}{>}\; \overline{f} + \overline{g} \quad \text{for } k \overset{*}{>} 0$$

<u>Theorem H-3</u>: Let $\overline{Z}$ be a basic solution of the generalized system for which the pair of conjugate variables (X_b, V_b) is at breakpoint. Then either a unique basic solution $\overset{o}{Z}$ can be constructed for which

$$\overset{o}{f} + \overset{o}{g} > \overline{f} + \overline{g}$$

or an infinite class of solutions $Z(t)$ can be formed in which

$$\overset{o}{f}(t) + \overset{o}{g}(t) > \overline{f} + \overline{g}, \quad \text{for all } t \overset{*}{>} 0$$

<u>Proof</u>: By Theorem H-1 there are two classes of solutions of the generalized system which can be constructed, and Theorem H-2 shows that

$$f(t) + g(t)$$

is strictly increasing on one of these. Using the notation of the proof of Theorem H-1 suppose that

$$Z_i(t) = \begin{cases} \overline{Z}_i - (S_i^T P_r)t & i \in B \\ t, & i = r \\ 0, & \text{other } i \end{cases}$$

was the class for which

$$f(t) + g(t) \overset{*}{>} \overline{f} + \overline{g} \quad \text{for } t \overset{*}{>} 0$$

If $S_i^T P_r \le 0$ for all i in B corresponding to columns of X or V, then $Z(t)$ is a solution of the system for all $t \overset{*}{\ge} 0$.

If not, let R be the set of all indices i such that P_i is a column from P_X or P_V which is a member of the basis and has $S_i^T P_r > 0$. Thus R indicates which of the columns of Z required to be nonnegative are decreasing as t is increased. Now choose s so that

$$\overset{*}{t} = \frac{1}{S_s^T P_r} \overline{Z}_s \overset{*}{<} \frac{1}{S_i^T P_r} \overline{Z}_i, \quad i \in R, \; i \neq s$$

There must be a unique s satisfying this relation for, if two of the quantities

$$\frac{1}{S_i^{\ T} P_r} \overline{Z}_i$$

were identical, the corresponding $\overline{Z}_i$'s would be proportionate. Then the matrix $\overline{Z}$ could not have rank $m + n + 1$ as required by Lemma H-1.
With this value for s, $\overset{*}{Z} = \overline{Z}(t)$ has

$$\overset{*}{Z}_s = 0$$

$$\overset{*}{Z}_r = \overset{*}{t} > 0$$

and each of the other basic columns of $\overset{*}{X}$ and $\overset{*}{V}$ are strictly positive. Hence $\overset{*}{Z}$ is a new basic solution in which P_r is in the basis, P_s is not, and

$$\overset{*}{f} + \overset{*}{g} > \overline{f} + \overline{g}$$

With these results rules may be formulated which remove the difficulty caused by degeneracy in the breakpoint tracing method. A little consideration shows that the succession of bases and corresponding basic solutions may be computed using the same recursion formulae given in Chapter 5. The problem arises in deciding which vector should be dropped from the basis in any given step. It turns out that sufficient information to make this decision is available from a basic solution of the ungeneralized system H-1 .

Given a basic solution Z for the generalized system and the vector P_r to be substituted in the basis, the problem is to determine s such that

$$\frac{1}{S_s^{\ T} P_r} Z_s \overset{*}{\lessgtr} \frac{1}{S_i^{\ T} P_r} Z_i , \quad i,\ s \in R,\ i \neq s$$

$$\text{(H-8)}$$

This may be done by examining the components of the vector relation H-8 in succession until a unique s is determined. The first components of the Z_i are identical to the corresponding basic solution of the ungeneralized system. For the remaining components of the Z_i, inspection of the generalized terminal-pair system shows that

$$\sum_{i \in B} P_i z_{ij} = E_{j-1} , \quad j = 2,\ 3,\ \ldots,\ m + n + 2,$$

where E_j is the unit vector with a one as its jth component and remaining components zero. Thus the quantities z_{ji}, $j > 1$ are the coefficients of the expansions of the unit vectors as linear combinations of the basis vectors. It follows that these quantities are themselves the components of the basis inverse vectors:

$$z_{ij} = s_{i, j-1} \, , \quad i \text{ in B}, \quad j = 2, 3, \ldots, m + n + 2$$

Thus the values of the z_{ij} are available from the basis inverse which is computed as a part of the breakpoint stepping procedure for the ungeneralized terminal-pair system. The steps required to determine the vector P_s to be dropped from the basis are given in detail in Chapter 5.

BIBLIOGRAPHY

1. Arrow, Kenneth J., Leonid Hurwicz, and Hirofumi Uzawa, Studies in Linear and Non-Linear Programming, Stanford University Press, 1958, Part II.

2. Boch, Frederick, and Scott Cameron, "Allocation of Network Traffic Demand by Instant Determination of Optimum Paths," Armour Research Foundation Technology Center, Chicago, 1958.

3. Booth, A. D., "An Application of the Method of Steepest Descent to the Solution of Systems of Non-Linear Simultaneous Equations," Quarterly Journal of Mechanics and Applied Mathematics, vol. 2, 1949, pp. 460-468.

4. Charnes, Abraham, "Degeneracy and Optimality in Linear Programming," Econometrica, vol. 20, no. 2, 1952, pp. 160-170.

5. Courant, R., and D. Hilbert, Methoden der Mathematischen Physik, vol. 1, Julius Springer, Berlin,1931 (Interscience, N.Y. 1943), pp. 199-201.

6. Courant, R., and D. Hilbert, Methoden der Mathematischen Physik, vol. 2 , Julius Springer, Berlin,1931 (Interscience, N.Y. 1943), pp. 26-31.

7. Crockett, Jean B., and Herman Chernoff, "Gradient Methods of Maximization," Pacific Journal of Mathematics, vol. 5, 1955, pp. 33-50.

8. Curry, Haskell B., "The Method of Steepest Descent for Non-Linear Minimization Problems," Quarterly of Applied Mathematics, vol. 2, 1949, pp. 258-261.

9. Dantzig, George B., "Maximization of a Linear Function of Variables Subject to Linear Inequalities," Activity Analysis of Production and Allocation, T. Koopmans, Ed., Wiley, N.Y., 1951, Chap. 21.

10. Dantzig, George B., Lester R. Ford, and D. R. Fulkerson, "A Primal-Dual Algorithm for Linear Programming," Linear Inequalities and Related Systems, H. Kuhn and A. Tucker, Eds., Princeton University Press, 1956, pp. 171-181.

11. Dantzig, George B., Alex Orden, and Philip Wolfe, "The Generalized Simplex Method for Minimizing a Linear Form under Linear Inequality Restraints," Pacific Journal of Mathematics, vol. 5, pp. 183-195, 1955.

12. Dorn, William S., "Duality in Quadratic Programming," AEC Computing and Applied Mathematics Center, New York University, 1958.

13. Feder, Donald P., "Solution of Nonlinear Equations," Wayne State University Computation Laboratory Summer Program, July 1956.

14. Fenchel, W., Convex Cones, Sets and Functions, Office of Naval Research Logistics Project Report, Department of Mathematics, Princeton University, 1953.

15. Ford, Lester R., and D. R. Fulkerson, "Solving the Transportation Problem," Management Science, vol. 3, no. 1, 1956.

16. Frank, Marguerite, and Philip Wolfe, "An Algorithm for Quadratic Programming," Naval Research Logistics Quarterly, vol. 3, nos. 1 and 2, 1956, pp. 95-110.

17. Hildreth, Clifford, "A Quadratic Programming Procedure," Naval Research Logistics Quarterly, vol. 4, no. 1, 1957, pp. 79-85.

18. Hitchcock, F. L., "The Distribution of a Product from Several Sources to Numerous Locations," Journal of Mathematics and Physics, vol. 20, 1941, pp. 224-230.

19. Jewell, William S., "Optimal Flow Through Networks," Interim Technical Report No. 8, M. I. T. Project Fundamental Investigations in Methods of Operations Research, 1958.

20. Klein, Bertram, "Direct Use of Extremal Principles in Solving Certain Optimizing Problems involving Inequalities," Journal of the Operations Research Society of America, vol. 3, no. 2, 1955, pp. 168-175.

21. Kuhn, Harold W., and Albert W. Tucker, "Nonlinear Programming," Proceedings of the Second Berkeley Symposium on Mathematical Statistics and Probability, 1951, pp. 481-492.

22. Lemke, C. E., "The Dual Method of Solving the Linear Programming Problem," Naval Research Logistics Quarterly, vol. 1, no. 1, 1954, pp. 36-47.

23. Markowitz, Harry, "The Optimization of a Quadratic Function Subject to Linear Constraints," Naval Research Logistics Quarterly, vol. 3, nos. 1 and 2, 1956, pp. 111-133.

24. Maxwell, James C., A Treatise on Electricity and Magnetism, Clarendon Press, Oxford, 1873, pp. 336-337.

25. Minty, George J., "On Monotone Networks," presented to the RAND Symposium on Mathematical Programming, March 1959.

26. Prager, William, "Numerical Solution of the Generalized Transportation Problem," Naval Research Logistics Quarterly, vol. 4, no. 3, 1957, pp. 253-261.

27. Tucker, Albert W., "Dual Systems of Homogeneous Linear Relations," Linear Inequalities and Related Systems, H. Kuhn and A. Tucker, Eds., Princeton University Press, 1956, pp. 3-18.

28. Weinberg, Louis, "Kirchoff's 'Third and Fourth Laws,'" IRE Transactions on Circuit Theory, vol. CT-5, no. 1, 1958, pp. 8-30.

29. Wolfe, Philip, "The Simplex Method for Quadratic Programming," Rand Report P-1205, Santa Monica, California, 1957.

30. Zoutendijk, G., "Maximizing a Function Subject to Linear Constraints," presented at St. Andrew's Conference on Mathematical Statistics, August 1958. To appear in Journal of the Royal Statistical Society.

INDEX

Algorithms
  for linear programming, 101-107
  for quadratic programming,
    104-107
  for diode-source networks, 56-71
  for network flow problems, 73-74
  for the maximum flow
    problem, 72-73
  for the shortest path problem,
    71-72

Basic solution
  of terminal-pair system, 81
  of generalized terminal-pair
    system, 171
Breakpoint curves
  defined, 159-160
  as terminal characteristic of
    networks containing diodes,
    39-43
  as solution set of a terminal-
    pair system, 159-168
Breakpoint tracing method
  for a terminal-pair system, 82-87
  for the generalized system,
    87-88, 169-180
  for an uncoupled system, 88-91
  for a reduced terminal-pair
    system, 91-92
  for the completely degenerate
    system, 92
By-pass method
  for obtaining feasibility, 98-101
  for linear and quadratic pro-
    gramming, 103-106

Complemementary slackness
  principle, for linear and
    quadratic programming,
    25, 143-144
  principle, for concave pro-
    gramming, 157
  in general programming, 12-17
  and the diode circuit element, 34
Concave (convex) functions,
    9-11, 148-152
  defined, 148
  properties, 148-152

Concave (convex) programming,
    26, 38-39, 153-158
  Lagrangian problem, 154
  duality, 26, 157
  complementary slackness, 157
  and nonlinear resistors, 38-39
Cone, defined, 12
Conjugate variable pairs, 81
Constraint qualifications,
    132-133, 135-137
Constraint set, 7
Convex hull, defined, 120
Convex set
  defined, 120
  defined by convex inequalities, 10,
    131
  polyhedral, 121
Current reduced network, 34-35,
    56, 93, 96-101
Current source, 29

Diode
  defined, 29-31
  and complementary slackness, 34
Diode-source networks
  nonredundancy assumptions, 53-54
  existence conditions, 54-55
  algorithms for solving, 56-71
Duality
  theorem, for linear and quadratic
    programming, 23-25, 141
  theorem, for concave program-
    ming, 157
  and conservation of energy, 34, 93
  in ordinary minimization, 21-23
  topological, for diode-source
    networks, 51
Degeneracy in the breakpoint
    tracing method, 81, 87, 169

Electrical devices
  current sources, 29
  voltage sources, 29
  diodes, 29-31
  resistors, linear, 31
  resistors, nonlinear, 38-39
  transformers, 31
Electrical models for
  terminal-pair system, 78-80